STILL NO PROBLEM HERE

STILL NO PROBLEM HERE

Chris Gaine

Trentham Books

First published in 1995 by Trentham Books Limited

Trentham Books Limited
Westview House
734 London Road
Oakhill
Stoke-on-Trent
Staffordshire
England ST4 5NP

British Cataloguing in Publication Data
A catalogue record for this book is available from the British Library.

ISBN: 1 85856 013 6

Designed and typeset by Trentham Print Design, Chester and printed in Great Britain by BPC Wheatons Limited, Exeter

CONTENTS

To Adam and Luke

PREFACE

One of the real rewards of having been involved in anti-racist work is the number of remarkable people I have met and worked with, sometimes over long periods, sometimes only fleetingly. It would be invidious to single out a few, but I want to thank and pay tribute to the resilience, courage and often humour of you all.

Chris Gaine
January 1995

Chapter 1

There aren't many of them here so there isn't a problem...

In 1975 I began teaching in the integrated humanities department of an 11-18 comprehensive which would in the 1990s be called 'progressive', situated in an almost entirely white area. It was taken for granted by the department that unfavourable racial stereotypes should not be presented to children, and my colleagues would surely have expressed disapproval of racist remarks. Were we all still there today we might be more sophisticated: a unit for year eight on India which I produced contained items I would now see as reproducing simplistic stereotypes, and our year eleven material on development/underdevelopment must have told many pupils that (black) people in poor countries are 'thick'. That aside, however, and given that we were learning, we were quite consciously trying to create a non-Eurocentric curriculum.

In my second year of teaching I was at a meeting set up by our local Council for Racial Equality, listening to a speaker talking about education. It is something of an injustice to the speaker, although not a major one, to summarise his message as 'present other cultures favourably in school and kids will be more appreciative of the value of others' cultures, and

1

this will diminish racism.' This has come and gone as a familiar stance over the years in multi-ethnic as well as largely white schools, and would generally be referred to as 'multiculturalism'. It struck me forcibly then that I already knew it did not work. It may have a part to play, but to hope that by some process of osmosis, ideas about cultural relativity or knowledge about Ramadan will transform the views on 'race' of many white schoolchildren is to hope for far too much. This latter stance might be referred to today as antiracist.

Some people reading this will not be convinced that there is anything particularly amiss with the racial attitudes of white schoolchildren, so I want to try and demonstrate something of the attitudes about 'race' of what I take to be typical white pupils in largely or entirely white areas. It is these attitudes which must be our starting point and not the presence or proportion of minority ethnic groups in our schools.

Attitudes in schools in white areas

I would like to point initially to the evidence from student teachers in my own college. In a recurring exercise with first year BEd students I ask them to write on a card (anonymously) what they have heard about black and Asian people. They know that their cards will be shuffled and read out by someone else in the group, so they do not have to 'own' what they write, and the point is stressed that they should write what they have heard, not necessarily what they believe. The results are always very similar: what they have heard is strikingly uniform and strikingly negative. It might be argued that the situation predisposes the students to write something negative, though in fact several often express embarrassment or discomfort at doing so and especially at reading them out, even more so if there are black or Asian tutors or students present. Several say afterwards that they realised what I was expecting to hear and really tried to think of something different, but without success.

There are recurrent themes. In one batch of 50 cards the distribution was as follows, indicated by typical key expressions:

'They should go back to where they came from'	21
'If they come over here they should accept our ways'	13
'They're just different, they don't belong here'	10
'They smell'	10

'They're violent, they cause trouble'	9
'They are thick'	8
'They take all the jobs'	7
'They're scroungers, they're lazy'	7
'They have funny food'	6
'There's to many of them'	4
'They're dirty'	3
'They have loads of kids'	2
'They're good at sport'	2
'They're good at dancing'	2
'They lower standards in the schools'	1
Miscellaneous negative	13
Miscellaneous positive	1

65 mentions were made by 23 students of abusive names black or Asian people are called.

It can be seen from this list that the idea of black people being unwelcome is linked most of all with the notion of them as troublemakers and with perceived difficulties about 'difference'. Other connections are less patterned, but repeat stereotypes that are at least forty years old.

I am not saying that the students themselves believe all these things. The point I am making is that these 18 and 19 year-olds have for the most part grown up in the home counties, in towns like Worthing, Winchester and Bexhill on Sea, and they write what they have heard. They write the expressions, ideas and stereotypes that have surrounded them all their lives, spelling out the constructions of black and Asian people which have been available to them. How much they believe them, resist them, or combat them is a different question; our problem is that in the 1990s these comments still reflect the climate in which they have grown up.

There is little published work on student teachers' racial attitudes. Richards (1984) discovered some flippancy in the way the issue of 'race' was regarded, as did Cole (1992) who asked some specific questions about post-war immigration. In the latter case the following disposition towards black people emerged:

tolerant	13
neutral/confused/not relevant to our analysis	19
unintentionally racist	8
intentionally racist	21

Siraj-Blatchford (1990) conducted a survey of the experiences of black students in initial teacher education. While much of her attention is devoted to institutional treatment, there are some indications of negative messages from other, white, students.

Moving down the age range to those still at school, research in my own school in the mid-eighties revealed powerful negative sentiments (detailed in Gaine, 1987). Briefly, when asked to write about 'black and coloured (sic) people in Britain' (amongst other things, so the real focus was not obvious) the mixed ability class was divided almost equally in their views, though the majority expressed feelings which were predominantly negative.

Few are neutral or non-committal, the topic is clearly one to have an opinion about, and quite a strong opinion. Key themes emerge: complete ignorance about colonial history; a conviction that most black and Asian people are on social security; a belief that black and Asian immigration and a very high birth rate has produced a housing shortage. Jobs are frequently mentioned, so is conflict, crime, language and religion, the majority being unable to distinguish between Pakistanis (nearly all Muslims), and Indians (in their town nearly all Sikhs). This is underpinned by massive over-estimates of the numbers of black and Asian people in Britain and the solution of racial conflict by the removal of the victims is a depressingly common proposal. Three examples capture the flavour of many:

> I think some of the white people don't like the coloured people then they get causing trouble. The coloured people shouldn't be allowed into Britain, they have their own place and they cause trouble when they are here. The coloured people wouldn't like it if us white people went over there to live. I think Pakistanis are horrible people.

> Really, I don't mind black people in Britain as most don't hurt us in any way. Though some people are a bit prejudiced I don't mind them over here as long as there isn't many of them. If anything it's the black race that really get the pounding as some aren't allowed in pubs or to join in some activities. So, as long as there is a certain amount of them I think white people will always rule this country. Though there is a danger of black people having families and the children, because of growing up in England, will stay.

> Many people are against coloureds and also against blacks. There is
> a lot of people who would like to see coloureds and blacks chucked
> out of this country. They always stir up too much trouble and then
> don't like being punished for it. Every coloured person likes and
> wants everyone to give them what they want when they want it. The
> Pakistanis always wear turbans. The reasons for this is their religion.
> The Pakis have a very strong religion. Most of them are friendly but
> you get the odd few that are violent. They also do not get married
> normally because marriages are all arranged. Also they are pigs.

It is striking how often their comments begin with apparent goodwill and
good intentions and later combine these with confused bigotry. Perhaps
they begin by writing what they expect teacher to want, then give in to
what they really want to say, or perhaps the brief period of thinking and
writing reminded them of the scale of our difficulties and so they dive for
simple explanations and simple solutions. On the other hand, as I suggest
below and more optimistically, they may literally be in two minds and not
know what to think...

Such writings have been collected from many of the shire counties of
England. From Cornwall to Cumbria the similarities are striking. None of
what they write can conceivably be first hand experience. The young
people who write such things are misinformed, not ignorant — and there
is no obvious correlation with 'ability'. I use the word 'misinformed' since
these are not random, chance misconceptions but patterned, learned,
stereotyped beliefs. They *are* informed of the things they believe, but they
are wrong, and their education has often failed them on all the common
themes they raise because it has not challenged them or engaged with such
myths in any systematic way.

In some largely white schools racial ideas take on much more salience,
for instance in some areas of London. Yet the stereotyped view of skinhead
gangs recruited by the far Right does not fit the complex picture described
by, for instance, Cohen (1992) or the *Sagaland* study of Thamesmead
(Institute of Education, 1992):

> The recognition of the confusions within and the sources of the racial
> attitudes we encountered amongst 10-14 year olds is ... very import-
> ant... We do not take the view that youngsters simply are or are not
> racist in their attitudes — although in some rare instances we did

5

encounter children with unambiguous hostility to all minorities. For the most part what we found was a blend of voices — the 'natural common sense' of inter-racial friendship, the 'all people are equal' ideologies of school and official morality, mixed in with accounts of black criminality, housing allocation unfairness, hostility to Asian entrepreneurialism or African-Caribbean youth culture (p.33).

If we move down the age range to ten-year-olds a less explicit or structured set of assumptions emerges. A simple but revealing exercise is to give each pupil a sheet of paper on which is the beginning of a story involving ethnic minorities: 'You are sitting at home watching TV when suddenly, there is a knock at the door. You go and answer it, and standing there is a ....' The next words might be 'black man', 'Pakistani', 'Chinese girl', 'Muslim', or whatever, though some children (or another class perhaps) should have 'taxi driver' as a control. Typically, between 50% and 60% of the class will write something signifying a sense of threat, fear, hostility, pity or perceived strangeness.

'Hello, my name is Sushi, could you please direct me to Chopstick Road?' ...... I switched on the TV when the news came on: 'Today we bring you the news that Mrs Harris that evil murderer has escaped from prison. At the moment she is going around dressed as a Chinese girl.'

...(The Indian)... then got hold of her and tied her to the bed. She was very scared and she didn't know what to do so she screamed and the Indian put some selotape over her mouth...

...(The black man)... reached inside his long grey rain coat, he pulled out a gun and said 'And where's your money...?'

...they found (the black man) upstairs in the loft and they put him in jail.

I asked the Pakistani 'Where do you live?' 'I haven't a home at all I am homeless could I stay here for the night please?'

When I got back the (black) pizza man had gone and he had taken the microwave.

These are not from negative, uncaring children — indeed the 'homeless Pakistani' above was immediately invited to spend Christmas with the family. The extracts are from a class in Cornwall, but I have very similar ones from an almost all-white Hampshire school where, on a previous visit, I had been struck by the secure and respected place held in the class by a Bangladeshi boy: classmates knew he was a Muslim, what this meant in terms of dietary laws, and that he spoke Bengali. Yet after a few moments' discussion of what they had written, someone who had relatives in London was informing everyone that they were virtually the only white people left in the capital. Oddly, too, when the class was asked in relation to the sorts of things written about Pakistanis whether anyone had ever met a Pakistani, several indicated the Bangladeshi boy. In the Cornish school, in a small town, there was even less first hand 'knowledge' (in fact some children asked 'What's a Pakistani?').

In discussing such written work with one group (again of ten-year-olds) they all agreed they knew 'nasty names for people with black or brown skin' but assured me they would not use them. I believed them, but was of course curious where they had learned these words. Almost without exception they told me they heard them from older siblings or teenagers just a little older than themselves. Were they telling the truth? Perhaps they mostly heard racist vocabulary from parents, but were perceptive enough to want to protect them? I do not think so, since pupils often raise differences between what they are told at home and school, but I can only recommend doubting readers to try something similar. Anyone who knows a class of ten-year-olds well will get answers in more depth than I can do as a visitor, but I do not doubt that the same general patterns will emerge.

What happens to these children between the ages of ten and fourteen? They learn, not for the most part from parents or in any crude way from the media, but rather from the culture and climate of the adolescent peer group they grow into, a set of negative stereotypes and a language which demeans and stigmatises black and Asian people as groups.

Little of this, however, is consistent and without contradictions. One might interpret the extracts I have cited as demonstrating what these young people really think but, while that is doubtless true of some, I have a more optimistic view. It seems to me that they don't know *what* to think. On the one hand there is a strong current of belief in justice and in treating

7

people as you find them, while on the other there is a series of knee-jerk responses that many have internalised about black and Asian people. They have an individualist language for someone they know or might imagine in their class, but no information or concepts which might enable them to construct different views about black and Asian people as a whole, other than those which circulate, by default, in the 'common-sense' they grow up into. Filling this gap is a real and achievable task for education, to shine a light on these contradictions and to make it safe for pupils to explore them.

There is a pervasive unwillingness in many adults to recognise that young children notice 'race', a belief in the innocence of children (see Menter, 1989 and Epstein, 1993 for good discussions of this). Troyna and Hatcher (1992) in a very perceptive and subtle study of mainly white primary schools, challenge this in charting the web of factors involved in upper juniors' racial attitudes.

The schools they studied had mixed populations, so they were not strictly comparable with schools with only a few Asian and black pupils, but they nevertheless provide useful recent evidence. They examine the salience of 'race' in young children's lives not solely through extrapolations from the political climate nor from counting specific kinds of incidents. They argue for a model which considers the key processes and forces, like the layers of an onion: interactional; contextual; biographical; sub-cultural; institutional; cultural; political/ideological; structural. They dwell mostly on actual interactions and incidents, distinguishing between 'hot' and 'cold' racial name calling: the former often taking place between friends in a temper, meant to hurt but having no commitment to their content; the latter being used deliberately to taunt other children 'for fun'. Both draw on (and arguably reinforce) pervasive negative ideas, but in neither case is the relationship between beliefs and behaviour simple and straightforward. Importantly, for many schools, they puncture the myth that co-operative looking playgrounds with apparently 'well integrated' Asian or black children are always all that they seem.

As regards racist beliefs, Troyna and Hatcher provide compelling evidence of racialised children's culture but not of widespread, systematic, coherent racist ideas. The key process was the interaction between the children, with all its characteristic intensity, drawing on the racial categories offered to it by the world as they experienced it in shopping, TV and the adults in their lives. They conclude

'Race' and racism are significant features of the cultures of children in predominantly white primary schools (p.195).

Evidence of negative racial attitudes in younger juniors and infants has been available for many years. In the first chapter of *Positive Image* (1979), Robert Jeffcoate outlines the experience of some primary and nursery headteachers of schools with small minorities of, mostly, Indian and Pakistani children. They began by doubting the research evidence on racial attitudes in young children presented to them by Jeffcoate, or at least denying its validity in their own schools. The account is worth reading in full. Briefly, he gets them to play the Balloon Game with their pupils, imagining they are cast adrift in a balloon and that it lands somewhere they would not like, and now write on..... They also tried other things, more appropriate to different ages, and although there was a complex range of attitudes shown by the children, many of the heads would, I imagine, echo the sentiment Jeffcoate quotes:

As the result of observation and some research I became aware that prejudice did exist among the children in my school. I should have said quite firmly before my participation in the project that this was not so' (1979, p.12).

This is old evidence, and may have cut some ice with readers in 1979, but there is an argument that things have changed in the 1990s, not least because of the increased awareness even in largely white areas that Britain is 'multicultural'.

Accounts from some of my students in Sussex primary schools scarcely bear this out. One, a black woman, on entering her teaching practice class for the first time, heard from a seven-year-old 'Oh God, it's a wog'. Another left in a Year 1 book corner some early readers that included illustrations of black children, and a running tape recorder, only to find a range of comments which the six-year-olds apparently knew were better not made in front of a teacher. Another happened to have some charity Christmas cards depicting Jesus, Mary and Joseph with dark skin, which prompted a discussion among a handful of nine-year-olds about 'Pakis taking over everything, even Christmas.'

Neither would the experience of isolated or solitary black pupils in primary schools confirm the view that the 1980s brought about a marked change. Akhtar (1986), for instance, was spurred into researching the issue by her five-year-old coming home from school in Norwich declaring that he wanted a white baby '...because I don't want a brown baby'. She found routine, commonplace name-calling and bullying in primary schools, '...a quiet erosion of identity and self-esteem, brought about by nice white children on nice brown children.' Here is Troyna and Hatcher's 'cold' abuse.

There are also accounts from black young people which partly account for their low representation in initial teacher education: having experienced schooling where they felt partially excluded (at best) they did not wish to prolong the experience as teachers (Singh, 1988; Siraj-Blatchford, 1992).

It is worth saying that this state of affairs received some official recognition in the early and mid 1980s. The Rampton (later Swann) Committee was gathering its information and provided some compelling evidence from different LEAs about the racial attitudes of white children:

(A)... major conclusion which we feel must regrettably be drawn from the findings of this project, is in relation to the widespread existence of racism, whether unintentional and 'latent', or overt and aggressive, in the schools visited... The project revealed widespread evidence of racism in all the areas covered, ranging from unintentional racism and patronising and stereotyped ideas about ethnic minority groups combined with an appalling ignorance of their cultural backgrounds and life styles and of the facts of race and immigration, to extremes of overt racial hatred and 'National Front' style attitudes...
(DES, 1985, p.234).

Not to do something about this, Swann argues, 'constitutes a fundamental mis-education' (p.36).

Pupils are misinformed and intolerant about many things, but my thesis here is that they are not simply misinformed but dangerously so. If statements that Britain is a multicultural society are to have any real meaning then these findings — taken from a range of largely white schools from the West Midlands to Cornwall, from Norfolk, Wiltshire and the Home Counties — have to be taken as giving clear imperatives for the curriculum.

Teachers' reactions

Before the reader goes off to try and get responses like those I have reported here for her- or himself I would like to issue a warning: even if similar views are revealed, many colleagues in the same school, teaching the same children, simply will not believe that significant levels of hostility exist. Their resistance seems to me to be for one or a combination of five reasons.

First, colleagues may not have examined their own assumptions and preconceptions about 'race', immigration, and prejudice, so the things pupils say might not grate on their ears the way they would on others'. For those who do not consider this issue important, pupils' attitudes are simply part of the background noise; they do not register.

Second, teachers are generally aware that this can be an explosive issue and not easy to handle in a classroom, or fear that doing so 'will make things worse.' An HMI document based on meetings held in five LEAs found that

> ...there was general agreement that race relations in schools were a matter of considerable concern, and that there was a need to respond to this concern (1983:p.3).

It also found that teachers may ignore things because 'racism is difficult and sensitive territory', and Swann often found the same. There has been considerable development work in many largely-white LEAs over the past decade, many whole school initiatives on 'race' in particular or equal opportunities in general, more interest in initial teacher education and a reasonable range of stimulus and support materials from publishing and TV, yet the fact remains that it is difficult, it does cause anxiety in teachers, and it this produces a powerful temptation to leave well alone.

Third, some will argue (with politicians', media, LEA, governors', heads' and parental support in many cases) that it is no business of the school to go into controversial matters of this sort. There is certainly plenty of ebb and flow in the 'official' support this issue receives. The Education Reform Act's preamble seems to say that such social concerns are the business of education; the later compilation of the actual curriculum tacitly said it was not. John Major said (with reference to Cheltenham's black candidate in the 1993 election) that racism had no place in the Tory party but, at the 1992 party conference, he said that student

11

teachers should not spend time studying the politics of class, race and gender. Perhaps some of those most anxious about opening this particular Pandora's Box would rather it was not there at all, so they deny its existence or its rightful place in school.

Fourth, teachers are usually telling the truth when they say they have never heard children expressing racist attitudes. Particularly in white schools it does not tend to arise as a public issue in chemistry, or typing, or when doing minibeasts. I always used to be struck by reactions to Grange Hill, not its 'race' content specifically but the fact that pupils seemed to like it while teachers seldom saw it as anything but an annoying travesty of school life. So it is, from the teachers' point of view, but for large numbers of children school is the backdrop against which they act out the important things in their lives: friendships, crises, group values, conflicts. The important things happen between lessons, in Grange Hill and in real schools, and we teachers are seldom privy to this world.

Fifth, teachers in white areas often point to the small numbers of Asian or black children in the school as indications that there is 'no problem'. 'Jasvir is very well integrated,' 'Carol was elected class representative,' 'Balvinder's best friend is a white girl' and so on. In fact this is entirely beside the point. Children (and adults) are easily capable of having positive feelings about individuals they know, but simultaneously holding generalised negative attitudes about the group that person belongs to. Individual black or Asian children are frequently told, 'Oh you're alright, it's all the others...'

All these reasons are important factors in people's resistance to the idea that 'race' has much to do with education for whites — for the ethnic majority. Teachers' anxiety about controversy, their often genuine unawareness of pupils' attitudes, the apparent 'integration' of the few black and Asian pupils, can all collude with our own unexamined prejudices to produce a pernicious conspiracy of inaction.

A task for schools?

Most of the teenagers in white areas are by no means as clear about 'race' as active members of the British National Party nor as firm and unshakeable in their views, but what attempt is made to shake them? Making them question their assumptions means we have to teach about the real world, about who they think poses a threat to them, the kind of responses they want to make to those perceived threats, and how they come to perceive them as threats in the first place. It means dealing with some of the unpalatable truths about life in Britain for black and Asian people, and thus being critical, which returns us to the point set aside earlier about what a school's business is.

In formal terms, there should be no argument that it is the business of schools to promote critical thinking about 'race' and culture. The Education Reform Act says a school's curriculum must prepare pupils 'for the opportunities, responsibilities and experiences of adult life' and a series of circulars are more specific. DES Circular 5/89 said:

> It is intended that the curriculum should reflect the culturally diverse society to which pupils belong and of which they will become adult members (DES, 1989).

From Policy to Practice in 1989 said the curriculum will 'certainly need to include ... coverage ... of gender and multicultural issues.' The NCC's Guidance Document on the Whole Curriculum (1990) states:

> ... recognition that preparation for life in a multicultural society is relevant to all pupils, should permeate every aspect of the curriculum ... and schools are encouraged... to foster a climate ....in which positive attitudes to ... cultural diversity are actively promoted.

The NCC's 1990 Guidance on Education for Citizenship recommends that pupils examine '...the origins and effects of racial prejudice in British and other societies.'

At the same time, the details of the National Curriculum have turned out to be less than helpful. Whatever teachers may wish to do it is not hard to understand why, in 11 years of compulsory schooling, most schools avoid anything contentious about 'race'. There was a brief time, encouraged by the Swann Report, where this picture looked brighter but sheer content overload, let alone the degree of prescription, must have reduced innovation. I shall consider this issue again in later chapters.

The humanities are a low priority, and controversy a lower one still, and this book is partly to make a case for teaching about 'race' in Britain as part of the curriculum every pupil encounters, but more importantly it is to argue for a higher level of awareness on the part of educators about the significance of 'race' in people's consciousness. My argument so far can be summarised as follows:

a) Almost all pupils, in almost all parts of the country, have considerable levels of confusion, misunderstanding, learned misinformation and ignorance about 'race'. Many have high levels of prejudice and hostility. (Those who doubt this can test it.)

b) When faced with the consequences of racial hostility people often say the answer, and a better future, lies in education.

c) No-one will ever challenge the states of mind of the pupils unless schools do.

d) Multicultural education as it has been understood may well leave these attitudes untouched.

e) If schools do not take this on board more generations of pupils will leave with their perceptions distorted and hostilities misdirected, and black and Asian people will suffer the consequences.

f) The problem of white people's attitudes to black and Asian people will not go away, and neither will the trouble which results from it. If this is not tackled in the shires then nothing will change in the cities.

If it can be assumed that those reading this book at least accept that many white children do have attitudes which could be called racist, I would like to address the problem of what to do about it. Earlier it was asserted that the 'celebrating cultural diversity/respect for other ways of life' approach is largely ineffective: as Sivanandan says 'To learn about other cultures is not necessarily to learn about the racism of one's own' (IRR, 1982: p.8).

This has been hotly debated in education for the past decade, the debate interweaving with others about the unity (or not) of struggles for equality in respect of social class and gender. The next chapter tries to clarify some key ideas and arguments about 'race' and racism; chapter three puts the range of views about racial education into context.

Chapter 2

'Race', Colour and Revisionism

Academic and popular discourse about 'race' is often vague about several related key issues and terms. In my own writing (1984, 1985, 1987, 1988, 1989, 1990, 1993) I have always placed 'race' in inverted commas to signify that it is a problematic term, but use it with reference to, loosely, groups seen as distinctive because of skin colour referred to by the shorthand 'black' or 'black and Asian'. I have referred to 'ethnic minorities' and quoted terms like 'cultural diversity', while revealing in some research on children's attitudes an apparent hostility about religion or language. There is also the term 'racism', usually hanging in the air above any writing about 'race'.

All these words are embedded in changing and competing understandings which have been particularly contested over the past fifteen years in Britain. Three different themes and discourses intersect here:

— notions of 'race' as something essentially physical and biological;

— sociological analyses of how we can best understand the patterns of relations and politics which might be called racial or ethnic;

— changing decisions about how groups of people choose to define and name themselves.

15

There is also a related issue to do with anxiety about offensive terminology and the trivialising label of 'political correctness', not addressed here. I want briefly to comment on and try to clarify and connect the terms and concepts above. They are confusing to many who are not particularly involved in this area of work and contested by those who are, not least because their meanings are not static.

'Race' and Biology

There is a common tendency in sociological books to say the term 'race' has no objective or scientific meaning and should therefore not be used, though they seldom clarify why. It has social meaning, clearly, which I shall come to later, but it does not have the biological meaning many people think it has.

Over several years, I have examined the definitions of 'race' offered by groups of teachers and students, revealing considerable blurring of concepts from different kinds of discourse. Definitions tend to include notions of appearance and colour (biological terms), nationality (a political term), language, religion and customs (cultural/sociological terms.) For instance, when pressed, most people would loosely and inconsistently describe as a 'race': Italians; black people; the Chinese; Pakistanis; Scots; and Jews, and confusion ensues in the case of black Jews or Italian-speaking Sikhs. There is also considerable wooliness over what might be genetically determined (like cricketing or singing talent) and how this might be linked to specific populations.

To take this latter problem first, folk wisdom attributes more to inherited nature between generations than geneticists do. Many assumptions about inheritance between generations are fairly spurious ('he's good with his hands, just like his father'; 'she's naturally reserved, but then so was her mother'). Of course there could be a genetic component to these, but the nurture element is likely to be crucial too. This gets even muddier if we distinguish between physical attributes like strength, and psychological ones like placidity and 'being good with money', or (relatively) simple ones like a good singing voice and more complex composite skills like playing cricket or practising medicine. Some of these things are too complex or too new to be genetically encoded and passed on from parents to children. To claim such attributes as biologically based and to go on to claim them as genetically shared within certain populations goes far

16

beyond any scientific claim, and in any case is simply not necessary; there are obvious and ample cultural explanations.

Returning to the matter of an adequate understanding of the biology of 'race', I find that the majority of people still think of essentially different 'races' in the nineteenth century sense, carrying a package of characteristics which correlate *with and are determined by* skin colour. Certainly many of my students believe there is a series of significant and fixed patterned differences (genotypes) between human populations who look different (phenotypes). The most frequent 'evidence' cited is the differential performance of black sportsmen and women and their 'natural rhythm' on the dance floor. The tendency for centuries has been to 'read off' various characteristics from an obvious one (colour).

A survey by the Runnymede Trust (*Independent on Sunday*, July 1991) showed that 1 in 7 of the population thought black people were inherently less intelligent than whites. A study by Cashmore (1987) found ideas of this sort often articulated by his middle class respondents, such as a company director employing two hundred people:

> West Indian's intelligence doesn't seem to rise to that degree. Don't ask me why, unless it's that their initial intelligence isn't sufficient to absorb what's required (p.50).

or a Jewish surgeon:

> In spite of adversity, (the Jew) has triumphed. This, I suspect, is due to having a greater number of neurons, being brighter and learning to overcome adversity (p.58).

In part, this biological understanding of the word 'race' is still with us in common sense because it is still with us in academic discourse, but at any level it is more than simply untenable, it is misconceived.

A notorious debate took place in the late 1960s and early 1970s, sparked by Jensen (1969) in the US and Eysenck (1971) in Britain. Their central claim was that black people had genetically determined lower IQs, and though scientifically untenable it was politically irresistible, so it ran and ran. (It was resurrected by a special edition of the *Oxford Review of Education* in 1991). The Swann Committee engaged two Cambridge scientists to examine whether there might be a genetic component to the lower measured school performance of 'West Indian' children in British

17

schools. By careful analysis of the figures they found no statistical evidence which could not be clearly explained without recourse to biology (DES, 1985, pp. 126-148). What is more interesting, however, is that the question was framed the way it was in the first place: that those with Caribbean backgrounds were seen as a biologically different 'race' who might accordingly have measurably different IQs. What really makes them different is the social value attached to their skin colour, not the skin colour itself. And in 1994 *The Bell Curve* has raised the issue once again.

The key issue here is the frequency of gene variants (alleles) which confer particular characteristics, and why certain alleles tend to occur together. For instance, it is common to think of 'African' appearance as a package involving particular facial features, hair type and dark skin, whereas in fact these are determined by different genes which are not tied to each other and which therefore vary independently. Any group which has historically been relatively isolated in reproductive terms will share a great many gene variants, so on this basis it is almost inevitable that a West African will have characteristic tight curly hair and dark skin, but the hair type is not determined by the skin colour, or vice versa. In principle it is quite possible to have tight curly hair and pale skin (a combination found in a small percentage of Norwegians).

Other significant physical attributes do not correlate with skin colour. Blood groups, for instance bear little relation to superficially observable 'races': many Swedes are more likely to find compatible blood donors amongst Eastern Aborigines than amongst white Britons; transplants are as possible between a white Londoner and a Nigerian as they are between two white Glaswegians (see Dunn, in Kuper, 1975).

Thinking of a fixed racial package of characteristics tied to an obvious one like colour is especially flawed when previously separate groups intermix, like the intermixing forced on slave women in the Caribbean and the USA by white overseers and owners. In these circumstances reading off other likely characteristics from skin colour takes no account of the gene pool from which the father came. The phenotype of black Americans and African-Caribbeans is similar to West Africans, but the genotype is significantly different. So it is especially dangerous for Swann not to challenge Jensen's underlying logic that intelligence can be 'read off' from skin colour. As for some other old chestnuts, the variant of the gene which confers dark skin and brown eyes does not simultaneously

18

confer dense bones ('black people can't swim') or a type of tendon ('black people are suited to 'explosive' sports') or a special ability to boogie. White men can jump.[1] The root of all this lies in nineteenth century European science which had the task of explaining the rest of the world with which Europe was in growing contact and the balance of power within it. This was particularly the case for the colonial powers and the USA where a rationalist scientific spirit was increasingly contesting the ideological stage with religion (see, for example, Fryer, 1984 and Jordan, 1968). Out of this arose the crude division of the world's population into three main 'types': Caucasoid, Mongoloid and Negroid, and the belief that in some ways culture was determined by or at least related to these types. One clear survival of this was the widespread use until the 1980s of 'Mongol' for those with Down's Syndrome. This usage came about because nineteenth century scientists thought Down's Syndrome in Europeans was a throwback to an earlier more primitive form of human being, and that all Mongolians were in fact 'Mongols'. Some equally explicit survivals of nineteenth century ideas have already been mentioned, but there are many more: the British as naturally inventive, or inherently reserved, or resilient — 'this island race', the Jews as avaricious, the Gujeratis as good at business, the Latin 'races' as naturally, essentially, emotional or exuberant.

Physical phenotypes, taken alone, have no explanatory power in terms of social, cultural, historical or behavioural differences between groups of people. Indeed the classification and grouping of human phenotypes for this purpose was long ago recognised as being an explanatory blind alley by most human geneticists or biologists. As Troyna and Williams put it, citing the UNESCO Conferences of 1947, 1951 and 1964:

> The designation of the world's population into distinctive racial categories can no longer be considered a tenable scientific enterprise (Troyna and Williams, 1986, p.3).

What matters is not the physical difference — real or imaginary — but the social significance given to it. Van den Berghe offers this definition of a 'race':

> a group of people who are socially defined in a given society as belonging together because of physical markers such as skin pigmen-

tation, hair texture, facial features, stature and the like (Van den Berghe, 1984, p.217).

Though it is crucial to note that the physical feature may be in part mythical, such as the Nazis' categorisations of Jews (in fact, a Polish Jew is physically likely to resemble a Catholic neighbour much more than a Spanish Jew). The social value placed on skin colour categorisations is most starkly seen in societies with rigid 'racial' hierarchies: being ostensibly white is not enough. Physically a person may be indistinguishable from a group of whites, but if they are known to have one black great-grandparent then there are places in the USA where the 'one drop' rule would still apply. One drop of 'black blood' makes someone socially black. In *apartheid* South Africa ostensibly 'white' people were legally reclassified 'coloured' on the discovery of some piece of family history.

Thus while physical phenotypes per se cannot explain social, cultural, historical or behavioural differences between groups of people, the social importance attached to the phenotype explains a lot. It is a social process not a biological one which accounts for why black people in the USA earn far less per head than white people and for their disproportionate presence in some sports. It is not genetically determined better vocal chords which explains the number of male voice choirs in south Wales, nor is there an inherited package of abilities genetically programmed into English middle class girls which accounts for their overwhelming presence in ballet schools.

The significance of colour

In Britain there are patterned differences in the jobs, earnings and housing of white people and those of people with noticeably darker skin. In these respects, at least, there is evidence of 'race' as a persisting and significant social marker. Four key studies (Daniel, 1966; Rose, 1969; Brown, 1974; Smith, 1984) described in considerable detail a pattern of discrimination in these fields resulting in a persistent pattern of lower pay and poorer provision. In 1994 the Runnymede Trust produced a compilation of data from government sources indicating that this broad pattern remains. For example, Indians are twice as likely to be unemployed as whites, Pakistanis three times as likely, and black and Asian people are more likely to live in areas of multiple deprivation, measured by such factors as low average earnings, early school leavers, and overcrowded and poor quality housing.

Daniel's report provided the impetus for the 1968 Race Relations Act, and while Conservative Party conferences regularly hear motions for its repeal, we might reasonably assume that it keeps its place in the statute books because there is some agreement that a degree of discrimination persists. (The Runnymede survey in 1991 found that 38% of white people thought the law in this respect was 'about right' and a further 31% thought it 'not tough enough'. Runnymede Trust, 1991).

Lord Scarman's report after the uprisings of the early 1980s observed:

> There are indications... that unemployment among members of the ethnic minorities is of longer duration than that among the white population.... discrimination — by employers and at the work place — is a factor of considerable importance....

> ... ethnic minority groups... suffer from the same deprivations as the 'host community' but much more acutely. Their lives are led largely in the poorer and more deprived areas of our great cities. Unemployment and poor housing bear on them very heavily: and the education system has not adjusted itself satisfactorily to their needs. Their difficulties are intensified by the sense they have of a concealed discrimination against them, particularly in relation to job opportunities and housing (Home Office, 1982; 2.35).

(Notice he says 'ethnic minorities', though he is clearly referring to colour.)

Some of the material inequality can be explained by indirect discrimination or by what some commentators call institutional racism. The 1984 PSI study (Smith) revealed how systems of word-of-mouth recruitment or housing allocation by inappropriate criteria can result in 'racial' disadvantage without it being anyone's conscious intention.

In less material ways, too, one can see the social significance of 'race'. Harassment and racial attacks have been commonplace for years in some urban areas (CRE 1981; Home Office, 1989) and are recognised as an inter-agency issue (police, social services, housing, education) in several shire counties, Hampshire for one.

It is for all these reasons that 'ethnic' monitoring has been introduced in several private and state enterprises: the argument being that unless one knows the ratio of applications to successful appointments, allocations, promotions or student places, one cannot know where discrimination might be happening, and hence where to take corrective action. (Quotas are unlawful in Britain, but there is a good deal of mythology about some London councils only taking on black staff, however incompetent. I hear more indignation about these rumours than I ever hear about the routine, systematic, computerised but finally proven and admitted discrimination against Asian and black applicants to St George's Medical School (CRE, 1988) which was nevertheless admitting an above average number of black and Asian students.)

This section is about the significance of colour. I have mentioned 'racial' discrimination, and suggested that one strategy to combat it is 'ethnic' monitoring. Having already argued that there is no such thing as a 'race', what do we make of ethnic monitoring forms (why not 'race' monitoring?) which divide everyone into 'black' or 'white' and then into sub-categories like 'Indian' (CRE, 1984). The confusion identified earlier in many of my students is apparently just as evident in official documents, and indeed the 1991 Census got itself into an impossible tangle when it was trialling questions which mixed biological, political, ancestral and religious categories.

One partial way through this is to recognise that ethnic monitoring is predominantly 'race' monitoring without conceding that 'race' is a valid category scientifically, only that it is a real and significant category socially. The problem is that such forms necessarily ask applicants to self-assign, whereas the problem the monitoring mostly seeks to address is the way people are assigned by others. What Reeves (1983) calls benign racialisation is embarked upon by some authorities in response to malign racialisation.

Racialisation

By the early 1980s the accepted wisdom in liberal and left circles in education was that the key determinant of the kind of inequality we are discussing here was 'race' and more specifically colour. The underlying causes may have been economic, historical and ideological, but more than anything else what determined who received the worst treatment was skin colour. This became symbolised in the new use of the word 'black', beginning in the 1960s in the USA. The slogan 'black is beautiful' had been adopted by those of African descent as an act of linguistic resistance

> ...to rid themselves of the negative connotations of the word 'black'; for them 'coloured' is a euphemism, an apology for a skin colour which is linguistically and socially defined as undesirable (Gaine, 1987: p.218).

The article from which this is taken was written in 1983, and represented my own attempt to clarify this hazardous area of terminology. The article continues:

> Being unable to ignore or sweep away the social distinction white people had created, black people went for redefining its significance in American social consciousness. The same process can be identified in a modified way in Britain... let me suggest that the word 'black' has a limited applicability in the same sense as it has in the USA, namely a group of people socially defined not by themselves initially but by the majority (dominant, white) group. 'Blacks' are socially defined by derogatory terms, by the discrimination in, for instance, employment which we know takes place; by the conditions of the Race Relations Acts which were designed almost entirely with them in mind; and by the operation of the Nationality Act. Thus 'black' in Britain is a socio/political term; it defines a group of people who have in common certain relationships with society, ie. experience of racism, and it is widely recognised a such by 'black' people them-selves. Used in this sense, it is unlikely to cause offence, and there is a consistency in meaning even when referring to groups as diverse as Ismaili Muslims from the Gujerat via Kenya and British-born children of a Welsh mother and a Trinidadian father (Gaine, 1987, p.219).

This is not, however, as simple as I once thought. Banton (1987) is probably right when he says:

> My guess is that most white people in ordinary conversation would use the adjective 'coloured', whereas most white Labour Party activ-ists, most white social scientists, most white people in the mass media and most Afro-Caribbeans would make a point of saying 'black'. (1987, p.328).

He might have added that at the time most Asian people actively involved in the struggle against racism would also have called themselves 'black', especially if they were young, but for some this has changed. Even then, there remained many Asians, and not just older ones, who preferred to be called Asian or even coloured, not 'black'. I have heard this written off as a surviving post-colonial divide-and-rule mentality, but some, having no illusions about white attitudes towards them, nevertheless see 'black' as implying Africa. Others are suspicious of a word which tries to lump so many different groups conveniently together.

There are two issues here and neither has been static in the past decade. The first is about groups being defined by their oppressors, and the second is about what kinds of things become salient defining characteristics.

Racialisation is the process that happened to people who settled here from the Caribbean and the Indian sub-continent. From being simply 'people', or Muslim Mirpuris, or Sikh Panjabis, or Barbadan Catholics, they became immigrants and 'coloured' immigrants at that. They shared some aspects of a colonial heritage and the perceptions of inferiority which went with it, and they shared the bottom end of the British labour and housing market. They were the poorest and the least protected by institutions like trade unions (or the law). They were also readily identifiable by colour and it was in these terms that parliamentary debates, documentaries, the white riot in Notting Hill, research and the first anti-discrimination laws were framed.

This is not to say that hostility was not expressed in terms of culture, or cooking smells, or language, but it is to say that the primary axis on which discrimination turned was colour. In this sense it was racism in the most old-fashioned way, the attribution of essential and unchangeable differences tied to colour. Whatever he may have meant, it is my view that this is the resonance struck by Enoch Powell in 1968 when he said

> The West Indian does not by being born in England, become an Englishman. In law he becomes a United Kingdom citizen by birth, in fact he is a West Indian or Asian still (at Eastbourne, 16.11.68).

On the long road to combat this imputed primacy of colour, common cause was made between south Asians and African-Caribbeans as 'black' people opposed to the discrimination they faced. Gilroy (1987) calls it

...the unifying tendencies of racist activity which regards the racial characteristics of both 'Pakis' and 'niggers' as being equally worthy of hatred (p.39).

It was analysed predominantly in the language of the left, and 'race' was seen as a sub-category of class, a physically defined underclass, and 'racial' relationships and inequalities were seen as essentially class relations (Hall, 1980; Sivanandan, 1984). Benign racialisation took the form of policies, measures, and statistic-gathering aimed at reducing the discrimination faced through 'race', and became an important issue in urban politics and administration by the late 1970s. Gilroy (1987) calls it municipal antiracism. It responded to a crude categorisation and was itself necessarily crude; it made a key point but perhaps it is no longer enough. It is time, as Modood (1992) argues, to go beyond 'racial dualism'.

Ethnicity

The insistence on 'black' as a strategic political category is, in Modood's words defining people by their mode of oppression. In his view the differences, conflicts and changes within the 'black' population require that people define themselves by their own mode of being, what is most salient to *them*, not in the terms by which they are marginalised and dehumanised by *others*. Thus 'ethnicity' becomes important. An ethnic group is a group of people who share a history, key cultural features, such as religion and language, and a range of less definable customs perhaps associated with marriage, food and the like. It may be that they are distinguished by some physical features (hair, eye or skin colour, height, facial features) but this need not be universal or excluding.

Ethnicity is a mode of being, 'race' is a mode of oppression. Ethnicity is about how people define themselves and mark themselves off from others. In this sense Jews are an ethnic group, Panjabi Sikhs are an ethnic group, British Poles are an ethnic group, and loosely speaking so are the Welsh. This is not to say there are not sub-groups within these or that the boundaries are neat and tidy, but it is to say that they are self-defining groups smaller than the broad categories 'black' and 'white'. Some of them are likely to become more important than they have been in the past in politics and policy making, for instance in the provision of separate schools on religious grounds, or the uniting over the Rushdie affair of many members of two ethnic groups, Bengalis and Pakistanis, divided by language but making common cause not as 'Asians' or black people but as Muslims (not least, as Modood points out, because of a sense of 'besieged insecurity on the part of Muslims who feel they are not valued or respected' (1992, p.5. See also Modood, 1990).

If culture and ethnicity are becoming more salient, then clearly it is no longer a simple black and white issue. There are Irish people, Chinese and Jews who barely received a mention in much previous literature (though see Taylor, 1987, Runnymede Trust, 1994). There is not a homogeneous 'black' underclass; there are sub-groups enjoying a relatively good economic position and there are aspects of identity (like gender, sexuality or religion) which for some people are more salient than colour, depending on context and on how constantly they are positioned by others. Colour remains a key determinant of the kind of treatment people receive, not least in the street, but language, religion and culture all play a key part in their being defined as 'the other'. Crude myths remain and there is a clear imbalance of power and influence, but the picture is arguably becoming more fragmented.

Culture and the New Right

If Modood is right, and this trend continues, ethnic minorities might seem to be curiously in step with the New Right. The Right (with the exception of the storm trooper wing, the BNP) no longer rest their case on biology. They used to — at one time they suggested explicitly or in coded form that white British people were biologically, inherently superior, but this is no longer the intellectual basis for their wish to halt and reverse immigration from the 'New Commonwealth'. Their argument is now one of cultural superiority or at least manifest appropriateness. British culture is a precious but fragile evolution, the argument goes, and it should not be undermined or challenged by alien influences which are either less sophisticated or at best more suited to somewhere else (see Barker, 1981).

At the political level, clearly framed in cultural rather than biological terms, there is the interview with Thatcher during the 1979 election campaign:

> People are really rather afraid that this country might be rather swamped by people with a different culture and you know the British character has done so much for democracy, for law, and done so much

26

throughout the world, that if there is any fear that it might be swamped, people are going to react and be rather hostile to those coming in (TV interview, 30/1/78).

and the famous Falklands speech:

> There were those who would not admit it... but had their secret fears that it was true,... that Britain was no longer the nation that had built an empire and had ruled a quarter of the World. Well, they were wrong... The lesson of the Falklands is that Britain has not changed and this nation still has those sterling qualities which shine through our history (Speech to Conservative Rally, Cheltenham, 3rd July 1982).

Racism

If there has been this transition in the focus of and response to hostility, and to its legitimation, how then are we to understand the term 'racism'? In general terms we can define it as a pattern of social relations and structures, and a discourse (linguistic defining and positioning) which has specific outcomes operating against less powerful groups defined 'racially'. By this definition racism is clearly more than an attitude, and is manifested in advertising, news[2], documentary and fictional representations; in racialised 'everyday' language; in laws; in interpersonal encounters; in material indices like housing, health and employment; in definitions of mental 'health'; in assumptions underpinning the curriculum and educational policy at all phases of education, and finally in the different ways people conceptualise and interpret the social world. It also manifests itself in the way opposition or antiracism is handled, marginalised, trivialised, co-opted and contained, or undermined. I have been arguing that historically the definition of 'races' has been in terms of biology, though progressively through the 1980s a more 'cultural' and 'ethnic' rationale came to be employed. Some argue this is 'racialisation', but is it not the other way round? What is happening is the culturalisation of originally 'biological' categories. As Brandt (1987) warns us, 'race' has the tendency to be synonymous with 'culture' and to be premised with the assumption that:

> ... all races are ethnic groups and that these have an identifiable culture which is representative of the group as a whole (Brandt, 1987: p.96).

27

Barker argues that scientific racism has been superseded by the 'new racism', a belief that certain groups of people, usually national groups, have distinctive, inherent and superior ways of life which are threatened by outsiders. Logically, this ought to be called 'culturalism' or perhaps 'ethnicism' but it never is, partly because 'racism' has such power as a condemnation. Those of us opposed to them would not like the 'new racists' to get a more sympathetic hearing because their new name sounds more respectable. But there is another reason why it is still appropriate to call such views 'racist'. They are still essentialist: conceptually they still rely upon fixed and immutable qualities. Indeed, at times there is an explicit biological argument that it is 'natural' to feel a sense of belonging, of kith and kin, with those most like oneself, so the cultural sense of nationhood is grounded in the nation being 'of common stock' (see, for example, Scruton, 1980, p.68.) In this form the ideology still oppresses, so that culture or ethnicity become modes of oppression rather than modes of being.

Perhaps too much is made of any racism being 'new', since a good deal of it sounds just like the assimilationist views of the 1950s and 1960s. By the 1970s and early 1980s, there was a furious debate about how racism in education was best tackled. The liberal wing held that a focus on culture was the key, the radicals argued the real issue was not whether someone was a Hindu or not, since that was a mere smokescreen for biological racism. The New Right are now saying (perhaps we did not believe them before) 'No, the real issue *is* whether someone is a Hindu or not, because Hindus do not belong here, and neither do Muslims.' No longer expressed in biological terms, it seems to have become respectable to represent certain minority cultures as irredeemably alien. The educational implications of this view can, of course, be seen in the National Curriculum, over which the New Right had a not inconsiderable influence: British history, standard English, and mainly Christian RE. The question is becoming, not whether someone can be black and British (and a Conservative parliamentary candidate) but whether they can be Sikh and British? (For a detailed account of this conjunction of 'race' and nation see Gilroy, 1987, chapter 2.)

To conclude this section, I am arguing that the ideological core of racism is a belief in the superiority of one group over others. The 'others' are currently defined by a confused mixture of essentialist qualities rooted in biology and culture, or a confused amalgam of colour, culture, language and religion. The confusion will doubtless remain, and it is perfectly possible for the crude primacy of colour to reassert itself politically in right-wing action and policy. The apparent promise in the cultural argument that those who adopt 'our' ways will become accepted and equal was not, after all, kept in the case of German Jews: in the 1930s they were the most physically and culturally assimilated ethnic group in any European country.

...and Prejudice?

Racism is not just about attitudes. Although I have spent some time examining whether it is ideas of biological or cultural superiority which justify racism, it would be a mistake to think that it stops there. A common response to the evidence of the attitudes revealed in chapter one is 'Well, yes, but it works both ways doesn't it, I mean they're prejudiced against us as well aren't they?' Black and Asian people can be prejudiced against whites just as easily as the other way round, and indeed some whites feel that this prejudice is more openly displayed towards them than any they express themselves. Pakistanis can be prejudiced towards the Irish, Jews towards Indians. A key difference, however, is that these psychologically equivalent 'prejudices' have different causes and different effects. In general terms, (and without wanting to peddle a crude racial dualism) white British people's prejudices towards black and Asian people have their origins in our colonial past, our ancestors' subjection and domination of those peoples, and the beliefs which evolved to justify and legitimate this. Some of these beliefs are still common currency, and the currency remains valid because it is easily converted into today's coinage of declining Britain, anxiety about national self-image and identity, structural unemployment, economic uncertainty and the conscious and unconscious quest for a plausible 'cause'. Black and Asian prejudice against whites has its roots in the same history, but a different experience of it. Inevitably some black or Asian people harbour a generalised suspicion of whites, brought about by patterns of systematic discrimination in employment, housing, immigration law, policing, and the provision of services of all kinds, as well as media representation as ignorant, fundamentalist, criminal, or here illegally in the first place. For many, this has been their experience in Britain over the past 40 years, and colonial subjection for two centuries before that.

So much for causes. The effects of different groups' prejudices are even less equal, because black and Asian people on the whole do not have the power to disadvantage whites. To repeat part of my earlier definition:

> ... racism is a pattern of social relations and structures ... which has specific outcomes operating against particular groups ... in material indices like housing, health and employment ... in assumptions under-pinning the curriculum...

Of course I do not own the language or the word 'racism', but I would suggest that it is very unhelpful to blur the distinction between personal attitudes on the one hand and key features of how a society operates on the other, by using the same word for both. It is also unhelpful in a school context to apply this kind of analysis simplistically and suggest that all white people have power or all white people are racists. The Burnage Report makes this clear as does more recent work by Gillborn (1995): often the only power white working class boys have is power of the crudest sort — they are not responsible for the racist structures in which they grow up.

The significance of 'race' for schools

I would argue that because of the short and long term effects of the attitudes and beliefs of many, even most white pupils, the beliefs of many of them can be called racist. Our education system claims to deplore this. Further, I would argue that this is a matter not of 'ignorance' but of misinformation, and a consequent attempt by pupils as they get older to make sense of the world. The problem is greater than 'understanding other cultures' because while young people may think Sikh customs are 'funny', they are at least as troubled by the threat they think black and Asian people pose, for example: 'There are too many here', 'Why are they here anyway?' 'They take our jobs (and live on social security!)' 'They mug us,' 'They're always fighting the police', 'They're taking over all the shops.' These things are said and believed, in my experience, by the majority of teenagers, and less specific hostility and fear can be seen in much younger children. I believe it is against this kind of backdrop that they are dismissive or hostile about aspects of minority cultures and easy prey to populist ideas about 'race' and 'nation' (though of course Scruton's 'naturalistic' argument would put it the other way round). It is also worth noting that in 1984 Cochrane and Billig found that about 30% of white 16 year olds at school gave the National Front or the British Movement as their first choice political party, on the sole basis of their policies of forcible 'repatriation' of black people. In 1994 the British National Party actively recruits young people echoing such recruitment in mainland Europe, trading on anxieties about work and their future and seeking answers in mythical nationhood and easy scapegoats. Those responsible for education ignore this at their peril.

Notes

1. I am very aware of how often people have unexamined assumptions about 'natural' sporting and musical ability. In beginning to examine these assumptions I think the key place to start is with the point that skin colour does not necessarily entail a package of other characteristics. But in any case, there is much more variation than such conventional wisdom has it. All Chinese do not look alike; not all Africans have the same kind of facial features (contrast Ethiopians with West Africans) and very dark skin does not inevitably entail curly hair (neither Aborigines nor south Indians have it.) It is also worth examining the male line-up for the Olympic 100 metres in 1993. Many people comment on the fact that all the runners were black while apparently failing to notice the far more relevant physical characteristics they did not share: some were short, some were very dense-bodied and muscle-packed, some were long and lean. Of course it is no coincidence that they were all black, but it was social factors which brought them there, not biological ones.
2. Hartmann and Husband (1976) demonstrated that the dominant message carried by the national dailies about 'race' was that blacks = immigration = large numbers = a problem). Searle (1989), in reviewing three months' output from the *Sun*, argued that it provided 'a daily dose' of racism, directed mostly at African-Caribbeans but also at 'Frogs, Wops, Krauts and Dagos'. While contributing to the developing construction of a new racism founded upon a (mythical) cultural 'Englishness' it also reinforced old myths. Non-readers of the *Sun* may be surprised that in the 1980s it continued to represent Africa by images of cannibals and cooking pots.
3. I am grateful to Mike Sinanan and Debbie Epstein for their comments on earlier drafts of this chapter.

Chapter 3

Education and 'race' — the national climate from the 1950s to the 1990s

An Overview.

'Race' was not an issue which penetrated British educational literature very much until the early 1970s. When it did begin to surface it was mostly from what could be called a 'needs of immigrants' perspective. It dwelt on the perceived needs and issues in schools and authorities which had numbers of pupils identified in terms of 'race' — black and Asian pupils mostly. By definition, therefore, this early literature had nothing to say about white schools and white areas (Bowker, 1968; Hill, 1976; Morrish, 1971).

By the mid to late 1970s there were many factors forcing a review, forcing 'race' onto the educational agenda, and the ten years from about 1978 to 1988 saw rapid and much contested change. The beginning of that period saw rising unemployment, the first real decline in educational spending for over a decade, and the first large cohorts of black and Asian British-born pupils entering secondary schools. The secondary schools in question were increasingly comprehensives (there was a spurt from barely

50% of pupils in 1975 to 84% in 1979) and some of the philosophy of child-centred education was gaining ground. These different currents met in urban classrooms, perhaps most of all in London, and by 1978 it was being argued by some teachers (not to say many parents and pupils — especially African-Caribbean ones) that education was failing black pupils (see, for example, Dhondy, 1974, 1978; Redbridge CRC, 1978; Stone, 1981). One of the last acts of Shirley Williams, as outgoing Labour Education Secretary in 1979, was to establish the Committee of Enquiry into the Education of Ethnic Minority Groups (later the Swann Report). Its prime impetus was the mounting evidence of underachievement on the part of African-Caribbean children, so the agenda was set, not surprisingly, around schools' response to the presence of black pupils.

There is one significant exception to this general picture, born not of urban education but of child-centred education and some of the ideals of comprehensive schools. The Schools Council began funding curriculum projects in the late 1960s and early 1970s, and one of these was the Humanities Curriculum Project on 'race', with a brief to aim at all schools. Amidst much acrimony and controversy, in 1972 the Schools Council decided not to publish the materials, for several reasons. Some of the Committee were alarmed by the inclusion of 'expressions of extreme views'; there was concern that the variation of grammar in the extracts from community newspapers 'might bring the Black and Asian communities into disrepute'; and there was some comment about the overly high reading level of the materials (Stenhouse, 1982, p.8). Whatever the reasons for the unprecedented veto, it was suggested that research continue into methods of teaching about race relations in secondary schools, and the former team continued their work, funded by the Gulbenkian Foundation and the Social Science Research Council. (The Schools Council continued work with a different emphasis in the project 'Education for a Multiracial Society' between 1973-6, see Jeffcoate, 1981.)

The teaching materials from this work were never published, apparently because by the time they were ready in 1977 the publisher withdrew 'in the face of revised estimates and declining textbook sales' (Stenhouse, 1982, p.2). Many research papers did emerge: Parkinson and MacDonald, 1972; Bagley and Verma, 1972; Sikes and Sheard, 1978; Verma and Bagley, 1979; and finally and belatedly an overview of the whole project by Stenhouse, Verma, Wild and Nixon, 1982. The dissemination and the

34

effect of this work seems to have been limited, perhaps because of the non-publication of the teaching materials and the late publication of the main findings. It may also be that the method being tried as one model in the research was that of 'neutral chairman' (sic), and there are some indications in Jeffcoate's comments on the Project (1979) and Stenhouse's own (1982) that this made it unattractive to those most motivated to do any work on 'race' in schools, who were not neutral.

By the 1980s 'race' was firmly on the national political agenda. Though developments went at different paces in different places, there were urban uprisings in 1980, 1981 and 1985 involving mostly (though not entirely) black youths. There was considerable increase in central government spending (mostly through Section 11 of the Local Government Act). Williams' committee reported (DES, 1981; DES, 1985). The majority of LEAs adopted policies about 'race', tapping the willingness of government to fund new advisory and developmental posts (London tended to be perceived as the prime innovator, with some justice). This was all accompanied by a fierce community, professional and academic debate about what form 'racial' education should take (this is touched upon below, and thoroughly explored elsewhere: Brandt, 1986; Gaine, 1987; Massey, 1991). Broadening the debate to white schools was still, while in principle supported by many of those involved in the cities, in practice left to *ad hoc* initiatives.

By 1986 reaction had clearly set in, so that the ascendant mission of those concerned about 'race' was being counter-attacked by those concerned about it in a different way. Gradually priorities were shifted, initiatives were pilloried and marginalised as extremist and 'loony left' (Goldsmith's College, 1987), the ILEA was broken up, a National Curriculum introduced which in places explicitly countermanded some previous changes, and Section 11 funding was redefined as only available for ESL work and then cut. Woven into this latter phase, however, is the Education Support Grants scheme supporting development work in white areas. Born of a belated recognition by Swann in 1985 that there was an issue to be addressed in white areas (hence the title of the report, *Education for All*) and a working through of this idea in mixed LEAs with both largely black and Asian and largely white schools, it became a national priority area for development grants and for in-service training. By 1990 most of these reached the end of their limited term funding.

Ironically, the issue of 'race' reached the agenda in many white areas just as the debate was being foreclosed in the areas where it started. Indeed, it might be argued that the debate was not so much foreclosed as reversed, with ethnic minorities being again regarded as 'strangers' and defined as the 'other'.

Education and 'race': changing perspectives

Most commentators see the development of educational perspectives about 'race' in three or four phases (Troyna, 1982; ALTARF, 1984; ILEA, 1984; Mullard, 1984; Swann, 1985; Troyna & Williams, 1986; Brandt 1986; Massey 1991).

While 'multicultural education' is the term most often used to describe anything to do with 'race' and education, it is often used with no great precision. I shall only employ it with the specific meaning set out below, since I want to argue that terminology in this field has mattered a great deal. Words like 'race' matter; whether employed consciously or unthinkingly a preference for using 'culture', 'ethnic' or 'race' actually demonstrates the ideological underpinnings of any analysis or proposed action. The agenda to do with 'race' has not just changed, it has been a site of struggle; one conception of the issues has not generally abdicated gracefully in favour of a new and younger paradigm. Terminology is revealing of how we see society and the processes of social and educational change, and each new name for 'racial education' has been founded upon particular and different understandings of these things.

Immigrant education

When black pupils began to appear in British schools in the early 1950s there was no explicit policy about their presence. Kirp (1979) calls this 'racial inexplicitness', and argues that in contrast to the approach in the USA, Britain 'did good by doing little'. Yet the way these pupils were treated and the generalised practices which grew up to deal with them were the product of Britain's implicit assumptions about immigration, which were markedly racial.

The main assumption well into the 1970s was to do with assimilation: the role of 'coloured' immigrants' (but not too many of them) was to 'fit in' to an (assumed) monocultural Britain, to aspire to 'do as the Romans', to settle down and in the course of time to move up the socio-economic scale. Education's task, logically, was to do some of the formal training required for immigrant children to 'fit in': this meant English as a second language teaching for those of Asian background and remedial English (at best) for Caribbean pupils whose English was 'not up to Standard'. It was a logical corollary of these ideas that when the proportion of black children became 'too high' in any one school (defined in DES circular 7/65 as about one third) then they should be bussed into other schools: if they were the majority they would not be able to assimilate.

Since this view of the world was essentially optimistic, (held as it was at a time of industrial and commercial expansion), self-confident, (it assumed that everyone saw the present and the future in the same way as the burgeoning white middle class), and liberal, (problems will be solved with goodwill and tolerance), it had to hold that 'race' relations were, on the whole, good and would present no problems as long as black numbers could be controlled and black children could be conformed.

It also follows that this perspective saw little place in school for the backgrounds and cultures of the black children, nor for their perceptions of how they were treated. It may also be true to say that apart from some resistance to being unconsulted, unvalued and their children bussed, many 'immigrant' parents were sufficiently powerless and imbued with the same ideology to accept this assimilationist model.

Thus 'assimilation' was a policy, and although it was conducted in what Reeves (1983) calls 'deracialised discourse', it was nonetheless racial. One understanding of a policy (Richardson, 1983) is that it is a means by which resources are allocated and legitimacy given to the allocation. In this sense, there was certainly a policy about racial education in the 1950s and 1960s, and in this respect Kirp's widely accepted account needs modifying.

It would be wrong to present assimilationism as entirely past history among those working in the field. Indeed, in the 1990s it is still technically the assumption behind most of the direct government funding of racial education. Most specialist 'multicultural' centres and staff were funded by Section 11 of the 1966 Local Government Act, including an antiracist unit in Brent which became the focus of something of a right-wing witch-hunt (see below). The Act, administered by the Home Office, allows for provision to meet needs of 'immigrant' pupils which are either greater than or different to those of 'indigenous' pupils. The rules have over time been interpreted in ways which are quite different from the assumptions implicit in the original Act, but, as suggested earlier, this kind of language structures thought: one effect of having to use the term 'immigrant' in all documentation about Section 11 is partly to be seen in the persistence of the genuine belief that this is what racial education is about. (See also Dorn and Hibbert in Troyna, 1987; and Etienne, in Gaine and Pearce, 1988.)

Obviously I think this policy, implicit or not, is flawed, and I ought to say why, especially as it is now being actively recycled. It seems to me that the assimilationist perspective is not only misguided and indicative of a poor understanding of history, it also involves a good deal of self-deception in some and arrogance in others. To be specific, I would argue that it has six weaknesses.

In the first place, the concept of British culture is built upon sand. It is an interesting exercise to try and outline the parameters of this culture without excluding a great many people who are not post-war black immigrants. I have heard many attempts to do so, and invariably those defining it actually come up with a class culture, that of the middle class, or part of it. If not, then it tends to be either trivial (fish and chips), or debateable (the quality of the BBC, loving animals), or at too high a level of generality to exclude anyone (patriotic?).

Second, this perspective demonstrates a poor understanding of history because it pays little attention to what immigrant groups have nearly always done. In brief, they do not assimilate on a cultural level in the way the model proposes. Even where structurally, that is in class terms, an immigrant group has assimilated (and the USA, the usual reference point in this debate, provides few enough real examples of this), they have not assimilated culturally. This is true for the English, Irish, Poles, Chinese, Dutch, Italians, Jews, Spanish, Greeks, Koreans and any other ethnic group one cares to identify in the USA, and indeed it is argued by Gordon (1964) that their structural positions do not represent assimilation either.

Third, such a debate is unnecessarily theoretical, since if one looks at the actual curriculum, even those who staunchly defend the promulgation of British culture cannot defend the status quo. While it is easy to prescribe in general terms 'British culture in British schools', in every subject one finds examples where this prescription is broken (even despite, one suspects, the best efforts of the Right to influence the National Curriculum). History courses today have to touch upon the Romans, the ancient Egyptians, and even colonialism. English literature is not entirely defined by books written by dead white men. A good deal of secondary school geography is concerned with the 'third world'. Foreign languages by definition are not British culture (perhaps learning them badly is?). The social context of much of science is shaped by the USA. All this is not to say that much of our curriculum cannot be made less ethnocentric, but those who defend its present ethnocentrism might first like to justify the study of Tutankhamoun, Bach and Moliere.

Fourth, it needs to be said that this perspective has been tried and found wanting. Perhaps there are those who think we should have persevered for another 20 years, but for 20 years this set of beliefs underpinned much of what was done in racial education and it did not work. The demand for mother tongue teaching or separate schooling has not come from assimilated immigrants.

Fifth, we are no longer for the most part dealing with 'immigrants' in the Britain of the 1990s. It is part of Britain's problem about 'race' that it cannot shed this term, it cannot see black and Asian people as anything but irredeemably alien, but we cannot go on having 'immigrant' education policies for children born and entirely resident in this country. We have to examine more critically what being British means.

The final problem with the assimilationist, 'immigrant education' perspective, and the most difficult one for us to admit, is that the expectation that black and Asian people should assimilate into British culture (even if we could provide a working definition of it) implicitly assumes the superiority of that culture, or at least the greater appropriateness of it in the British Isles. For many people in Britain the phrase 'when in Rome...' seems to contain a self-evident truth but perhaps it does not.

It should be clear why many people regard this constellation of assimilationist views as both racist —because they have the effect of making Asian and black experiences and perceptions inferior — and inaccurate and misleading, since it reflects an inadequate and inaccurate picture of Britain's present and former place in the world. To promote an educational perspective which is both inaccurate and racist (as well as obviously outdated) is harmful to white people as well as to Asian and black people.

Multiracial education

Some commentators, notably Stone (1981) and Mullard (1984) have identified a second main form of racial education, 'multiracial education'. This, they argue, concentrated mainly on remedial measures for African-Caribbean children's low self-esteem, and in different ways they critique it. This debate is covered in Gaine (1987), though it is worth pointing out again the variation in terminology: Sarup's *The Politics of Multiracial Education* (1986) is actually about what most writers would recognise as multicultural education.

Multicultural Education

Multiracial education had a clear focus on black children. While there was never a clear break in people's motives or in their practice, there is nevertheless a distinction between this emphasis and multicultural education, which came later.

This perspective seemed to conceive of society as composed primarily, and most importantly, of cultures. Various assumptions might be made about the comparative and potential equality of cultures, but the central theme was of a plural social order. Cultures, according to this model, are generated by several things, often in concert: one of these is class, another is region, another is religion, another is ethnicity, so we may speak of 'northern' culture, or Panjabi culture, and these exist side by side in a plural social order, an order differentiated by culture rather than or at least as much as stratified by class (Craft, 1982; 1984).

This social theory underpinning multicultural education recognised that (mostly black and Asian) minority ethnic cultures are devalued, but argued that in principle this could be changed towards a diversity of equal cultures. The Schools Council, in their explanatory leaflet about the Council's initiatives in this field, stated that there is move in Britain towards

> ... cultural pluralism, which recognises that our society may be positively enriched by the presence of a variety of cultural patterns... successive British governments have firmly endorsed a policy of mutual understanding and respect for individual differences and cultural diversity.... The goal is a plural society where cultural groups can maintain their own identity, but where there are sufficient shared ex-

periences and values for social cohesion and sufficient understanding of each other's culture for stability (1982: p.2).

This document recognises that the goal it identifies has not been reached, and the reasons it gives for this are revealing of the underpinning analysis:

... assimilation is difficult to achieve for some cultural groups now in Britain. Many of these groups are loosely referred to as 'ethnic minorities'.... Skin colour and language differences make some minority groups visibly and audibly distinctive; differences in religious belief and practice may reduce social interaction and intermarriage. Groups which can so easily be identified and which may seem strange or unfamiliar are an easy prey for prejudice, hostility and discrimination (ibid. p.2).

According to this approach the necessity for multicultural education arose from strangeness, inadequate recognition and understanding of each other's cultures, and from 'prejudice'. Its remedy has been both summed up and mocked in the phrase, 'the steel band and Diwali' approach: import some 'ethnic' musicians and have some assemblies for the festivals of non-Christian faiths. Others have called it 'steel band and samosas'. It is summarised more formally by the ILEA (1984) and by Richardson (1985).

The Schools Council's perspective was shared by the Swann Report in 1985, although it used the term 'pluralism'. It recommended a critical perspective at times, and argued that the central curriculum point, especially in white areas, must be to deal with racism, but it nevertheless had a fundamentally psychological understanding of what racism is. (The nearest the report comes to defining it closely is in its second chapter, where it used it synonomously with 'negative prejudice'.) Its view of society was as follows:

We consider that a multi-racial society such as ours would in fact function most effectively and harmoniously on the basis of pluralism which enables, expects and encourages members of all ethnic groups, both minority and majority, to participate fully in shaping the society as a whole within a framework of commonly accepted values, practices and procedures, whilst also allowing, and where necessary, assisting the ethnic minority communities in maintaining their distinct ethnic identities within this common framework (DES, 1985, p.5).

41

I would maintain that it is the cultural framing of this approach which ensured it support. It did not mention 'race' and was not underpinned by any notion of class. Its goals were 'tolerance' for whites and integration for blacks and Asians. It took the issue of white racism seriously, but saw it mainly as an outcome of psychology or of ignorance. It therefore asked no really threatening questions. On the whole, too, it has to be said that it kept the urban focus of its predecessors. Whatever the intentions, in practice multicultural education was mainly to be found where there was ethnic cultural diversity to celebrate.

Antiracist education

By 1980 there were several writers arguing that the issues should be framed in terms of racism rather than cultural difference and personal prejudice, but it was not until 1984 that this dichotomy came to dominate writing, conferences, policy formulation and terminology. The term 'racism' was a key part of the Rampton report (1981) and thereafter became increasingly a focus in the journal *Multiracial Education*. Workshops at the 1983 conference of the National Association for Multiracial Education found they could not take a common perspective for granted (NAME, 1983), and by 1985 NAME changed its name to the National AntiRacist Movement in Education, amid heated debate and followed by resignations and disaffiliating branches. Though LEAs, especially urban ones, were increasingly adopting policies about 'race', ILEA became almost the only authority actually to call its policy 'antiracist'.

By this time the cultural formulation of the issues had failed to convince activists and educators on the 'front line' of urban education, if indeed they ever gave it serious consideration. As one slogan put it, they were concerned with life chances, not life styles. Sarup said a little later (1986) 'We don't have culture riots'; by that time the occurrence of large scale street confrontations by disaffected youth had served effectively to prioritise 'race'. The All London Teachers Alliance against Racism and Fascism, the urban, black members of NAME (as opposed to its historical membership of white ESL teachers) and the policy makers of ILEA and some other (mainly London) boroughs, were all seeking to define the educational inequalities stemming from 'race' in a much more radical way. This generally made a tacit or implicit connection with class. Chris Searle's *The World in a Classroom* (1977) is a good example of this, though the date demonstrates that this kind of perspective was alive some years earlier, and that the temporal sequence I am presenting is somewhat idealised.

Mullard and Stone dismissed multiracial education as naive about the effects of class. Multicultural education did not really recognise class as a factor at all. Mullard argued that racism can only be truly understood and combated from a Marxist standpoint and that, therefore, the only true antiracism is Marxist. Though it contained only one rather general chapter about education, the key book *The Empire Strikes Back* (CCCS, 1982) also aimed to give a contemporary Marxist analysis and to 'closely relate racism in all its contradictions to changes and problems within capitalism'. In this the CCCS and Mullard would be supported, at least partly, by many in the groups mentioned above such as ALTARF and socialist LEA councillors. The argument was that class and 'race' have different expressions and different power, but broadly speaking they are to be regarded as closely related (if not reducible to the same thing) in that they are part of the system of relations which shape and maintain British society. Each one is not an aberration or an unfortunate hangover from the past, they are profitable.

Several commentators and activists argued that multicultural education was merely a white response to black demands, a way of not facing up to the real issues and rendering unpalatable inequalities into cultural differences. Antiracism, Mullard argued:

> ... is concerned with the production of quite a different kind of consciousness than that with which it is in contest. Unlike multicultural education which seeks to produce a passive consciousness of cultural differences, antiracist education seeks to produce an active consciousness of structural similarity, inequality and injustice' (1984: p.33).

The educational practice thus recommended by antiracists was twofold: firstly to examine structures and practices, secondly to have a curriculum and a pedagogy which are liberating and transformational in the sense of making students critical of the linked inequalities which they experience. ARE was more likely to develop a 'left' view of society with racism within it, which might mean much more working-class history, project work on deportation campaigns, examples in maths taken from South African statistics, and the politics of food in home economics. Outside the class-room an ARE stance would also mean considerable community involve-ment, for example against the Police Bill, or in campaigns about racial harassment and deportation.

Strategies of labelling... Education for Racial Equality

Despite the unambiguous stance of ALTARF, Searle, and (on paper) the ILEA, other teachers and LEAs either were, or appeared to be, more cautious. One of the practical reasons behind the apparent dispute over terminology was simply tactics, the tactics of how to address an issue which was seen as threatening and challenging, and thus likely to provoke powerful opposition (see Gaine, 1987).

Whatever the pervasive level of racism in Britain it could not be argued that it is overtly and publicly recognised. On the contrary, it is often denied. Though there is a Race Relations Act (implying the legislators' belief in its necessity) at every Conservative Party Conference since the Act was passed in 1965, there have been motions calling for its repeal. These have been partly argued on the basis that the law 'makes things worse', that in time market forces will solve any problem, but also that there is not really a problem.

Denial may indeed be a characteristic feature of British racism, what Mukherjee (1981) and Twitchin (1983) have called 'liberal racism'. It is significant that in a public campaign about the placing of children in Dewsbury schools in 1987/8, the group of white parents involved were at great pains to point out that they were not 'racists' (BBC, 1987; Naylor, 1989). The point here is not whether they were or not, but that it appeared to matter greatly whether they were defined as such. The same thread can be seen in the 'Honeyford Affair' in 1986 (see Troyna, 1987). Yet as Gilroy (1987) and Tomlinson (1990) point out, this denial is made against a backdrop of implicit educational, media, and political messages of white superiority.

But if racism is not acceptable, then neither is antiracism, and educa-tional advocates of this stance had to protect themselves, their initiatives and their practices from attack. One obvious line of attack from those who denied racism was to impute 'other motives' to those who drew attention to it, and in this respect some antiracists provided easy targets. Mullard and Searle, and also Hatcher (1985) for instance, clearly identified them-

44

selves as on the left, and it was a simple (if simplistic) task for Flew (1984) to produce a paper suggesting that racism was not the real concern at all (it could not be, since it scarcely existed); 'racism' was simply being used as a Trojan horse in a class war. The same 'reds under the bed' attack was made upon the Anti-Nazi League in the late 1970s, though it was arguably a genuinely broad-based antiracist movement (Thames TV, 1979).

Faced with this kind of attack or its possibility, LEA officers, activists and local politicians had to be very careful of their language. The definition of racism Berkshire gave on the opening page of its policy was as follows:

> Racism refers to institutions and routine procedures as well as to the actions of individuals, and to unconscious and unintentional effects as well as to deliberate purposes. It summarises all attitudes, procedures and social patterns whose effect (though not necessarily whose conscious intention) is to create and maintain power, influence and well-being at the expense of Asian and Afro-Caribbean people; and whose further function is simultaneously to limit the latter to the poorest life chances and living conditions, the most menial work, and the greatest likelihood of unemployment and under-employment (Berkshire, 1983).

Despite its critical tone it is important to note that the definition, and the rest of the policy, implied that racism can be countered to the benefit of British society. It does not suggest the total restructuring of British society. (Swann, in commending Berkshire in 1985, explicitly said this is not what it wanted.)

Hatcher (1985) called this the 'education for racial equality' (ERE) perspective, reserving 'antiracist education' (ARE) for more radical stances. To some extent this is a matter of 'ideal types', notional pure forms and personal positions which do not exist in reality with such clarity. Yet while the distinction between ERE and ARE is perhaps more recognisable in a formal and analytic sense than in educational organisation or classroom practice, the distinction was crucial in local politics. While very embroiled in the politics of these definitions I wrote in 1987:

> It is hardly surprising that the formal statements of the ERE position ... do not overtly take a more radical stance, the whole point of radical and neo-Marxist critiques of them ought to be that it would be

impossible for them to do so. They are designed to get through political committees. ... the earliest of the ERE policies, Berkshire's, was passed by a 'hung' council, which meant it had to get Conservative votes. Bradford's, indeed, was passed by a Conservative council. The ERE position can be elusive, and usually has to take a stance suggesting that racism is not an inevitable and necessary part of society. But a 'weak' antiracist position is often argued by those holding a stronger one and who dare not say so. These people work in education, generally in or around schools, where with very few exceptions they deem it personally and strategically unwise to be identified as 'too extreme'. (There is, of course, an argument which says such compromises weaken the struggle and should not be made.) The best example of this is Mullard himself, who was involved in writing both the Berkshire policy and the ILEA's, and who now subjects them to a Marxist critique. ... in this territory many people are in disguise. Marxist antiracists call themselves multiculturalists, 'steel band and Diwali' types wear antiracist badges, and many people combat injustice without a watertight and coherent social theory (Gaine, 1987, p.37).

In an otherwise acute account of policies and the local state, Troyna and Williams (1986) seem to miss these strategic realities. They analyse the ideology of policies as revealed in their language, but do not relate them to the real political messages they had to convey and deny.

The following chart is an example of how difficult it was to distinguish ARE and ERE. It comes from an article by Richardson (1985), then the adviser for multicultural education (note the title) for Berkshire. The last column seems deliberately written so it can be defended from an ERE position while giving more than a nod in the direction of ARE.

For those who genuinely espoused it, the key feature of the ERE position was that it regarded racism as an isolatable phenomenon within society, not an inherent part of its structure. Thus, although racism could be seen as inescapably having its origin in colonialism and capitalism, it can still be seen as an ideology and a set of practices which can be analysed and countered separately from the structures of class.

ERE argued that racism and inequality should be addressed more centrally by the school curriculum. It wanted to give pupils a critical understanding of racism rather than hope for 'harmony' through goodwill,

ISSUES AND CONTROVERSIES IN THE SWANN REPORT: A MAP

Immigrants came to Britain to the 1950s and 1960s because the laws on immigration were not strict.	Ethnic minorities came to Britain because they had a right to and because they wanted a better life.	Black people came to Britain, as to other countries, because their labour was required by the economy.
Immigrants should integrate as quickly as possible with the British way of life.	Ethnic minorities should be able to maintain their language and cultural heritage.	Black people have to defend themselves against racist laws and practices, and to struggle for racial justice.
There is some racial prejudice in Britain, but it's only human nature, and Britain is a much more tolerant place than most other countries.	There are some misguided individuals and extremist groups in Britain, but basically our society is just and democratic, and provides equality.	Britain is a racist society, and has been for several centuries Racism is to do with power structures more than with the attitudes of individuals.
It is counter-productive to try to remove prejudice — you can't force people to like each other by bringing in laws and regulations.	Prejudice is based on ignorance and misunderstanding. It can be removed by personal contacts and the provision of information.	'Prejudice' is caused by, it is not the cause of, unjust structures and procedures. It can be removed only by dismantling these.
There should be provision of English as a Second Language in schools, but otherwise 'children are all children, we should treat all children exactly the same' — it is wrong to notice or emphasise cultural or racial differences. Underachievement is caused by home background and culture.	Schools should recognise and affirm ethnic minority children's background, culture and language . . . celebrate festivals, organise international evenings, use and teach mother tongues and community languages, teach about ethnic minority history, art, music, religion, literature.	Priorities in education are for there to be more black people in positions of power and influence — as heads, senior teachers, governors, education officers, elected members; and to remove discrimination in the curriculum, classroom methods and school organisations; and to teach directly about equality and justice and against racism.

and it sought to rethink structures and practices which diminish life-chances for Asian and black people. ERE refined the notion of 'institutional racism', as the network of (sometimes) unexamined assumptions, procedures and practices in British society which have the effect of disadvantaging Asian and black people and maintaining white power. In practice this meant, for instance, positive action on recruitment, monitoring job appointments and being prepared to act upon the results, and having enforceable sanctions for racist behaviour.

In addition, and crucially, ERE argued for work in white areas. The 'multicultural' conception of racial education had never really caught on outside the cities, where there was not much face to face (ethnic) cultural diversity to celebrate. The issue hardly had the urgency for tomorrow's lessons that it did in central Birmingham, so in practice it seldom seemed to provide enough of a motive to touch the curriculum, let alone examine racism. The ERE stance suggested, however, that there was the possibility of a short cut being taken through the educational development of the big conurbations. Without the distraction, so to speak, of the Asian and black communities and the various understandings of their needs in school, it would be possible to look directly at the needs of white pupils.

The late 80s — one step forward, two steps back?

The distinction which I was concerned to make as an activist in the 1980s was not widely taken up. The debate continued in perhaps a rather sterile way between the increasingly stereotyped 'multiculturalists' and 'anti-racists', though a clear stance about racism became a more overt part of language work, particularly the advocacy of bilingual support (see, for instance, Singh, 1988). The late 1980s saw two almost contradictory developments. The first was the emergence of white-areas development work (ESG Projects and in-service grants) with central government funding (and hence legitimacy) as an eventual outcome of Sir Keith Joseph's response to the Swann Report. Simultaneous with this in some of the more 'aware' white LEAs was the adoption of policies and the appointment of senior staff to implement them, and gradually other LEAs followed them. The second was the right wing reaction to the developments outlined so far. Clearly, what the phrase 'education for all' ought to mean was open to quite different interpretations.

In 1985 Swann had called the final report of the Committee of Enquiry into the Education of Children from Ethnic Minority Groups, *Education for All*, partly in recognition of what two of their researchers had found in largely white areas (Matthews and Fallows, Chapter 5 Annexes C and D of the Report).

Because of DES access to an early draft of the Report, in 1984 Keith Joseph (then Education Secretary) approved the prioritising of 'multicultural' work in white areas under the Education Support Grants Scheme (ESG). This provided 70% of the funds centrally, and LEAs had to bid for projects lasting from one to five years. Twenty one 'areas of national importance' were prioritised, of which 'Educational Needs in a Multi-ethnic Society' was one. If LEAs made bids for prioritised areas they were more likely to be successful, and this clearly helped to get the issue on the agenda.

I discuss these projects and other LEA developments in a later chapter. For the moment it is worth noting that the issue of terminology discussed earlier was again evident in these projects' titles. Although by 1988 it was clear that the *raison d'etre* of many of them was to change the attitudes of white pupils, the language even as cautiously used by Swann had been changed. In the list of projects supplied by the DES in 1989 the words 'racism' and 'antiracist' do not appear at all, being codified instead as 'promoting racial harmony' or 'preparing all pupils for life in a multi-ethnic society' or 'increasing awareness' or 'reducing racial tension' (see Tomlinson, 1990, pp.106-115).

Other developments which arguably had some effect, and certainly, in time, produced a reaction, were the appointment of specialist advisers/inspectors and the mounting by largely white LEAs of in-service courses.

The Emerging Right-Wing Reaction

The above developments in white areas, could if taken alone, be seen as evidence of a changing climate about 'race' in education. It is reasonable to see them as a progressive development from the struggles of urban LEAs to come to terms with the educational issues arising from the presence of black and Asian pupils. Meanwhile, however, a reaction was developing, and an increasingly concerted opposition made itself felt from the mid 1980s onwards.

As indicated earlier, by the beginning of the 1980s some fault lines were beginning to appear in urban education. Real spending was being cut by both the outgoing Labour government in 1979 and by Labour LEAs in the 1980s. The new Conservative government did not reverse this. The first cohorts of largely British-born black and Asian youngsters were established in secondary schools, and these secondary schools were now predominantly comprehensive, and affected to some extent by the philosophy of child-centred education (see Plowden 1967). As one complex outcome of this complex situation some LEAs, particularly in London, were evolving explicit policies about 'race' and inequality.

Some of the contributors to the Black Papers of the early 1970s must have felt that their unheeded warnings of their worst fears were coming true. Whatever else was happening, the face of British urban secondary education was undergoing considerable changes. In addition, there may have been those who were not overly concerned with urban schools where black, Asian and working class pupils were schooled, but who began to be alarmed when 'Swann and the Spirit of the Age' (Pearce, in Palmer, 1986) looked like it might spread to the 'white highlands'. A DES report, chaired by an Establishment Lord and accepted by the then Education Secretary may have been seen as a much more considerable threat.

In the early years of what will probably become known as the Thatcher Era there emerged several right-wing policy bodies ('think tanks') and pressure groups. The Freedom Association was one of the earliest, founded in 1975 just as Thatcher became Conservative leader, though it was not until much later that it became involved in educational issues. The Social Affairs Unit was an offshoot of the older Institute of Economic Affairs. The Centre for Policy Studies was established by Thatcher herself with Keith Joseph, as a promoter of 'new' right-wing ideas.

The growing focus on education was part of a larger Conservative project of constructing a new nationalism. As recounted earlier, some commentators such as Rushdie (1983) as well as Gilroy (1987) and Hall (1988) have argued that this nationalism depended on defining the 'British' or even the English by who is excluded. As Tomlinson says:

> The Victorian conjunction between race and nation is still apparent in the presentation of the British nation as biographically and culturally exclusive and monocultural (Tomlinson, 1990, p.34).

50

In the 1980s, beginning in about 1982 when the developments outlined
above were well established, the groups began to multiply. The *Salisbury
Review* was first published in 1982. Ostensibly a journal, it had a group
of frequent contributors which overlapped in membership with the CPS
and the newer Hillgate Group, the Parental Alliance for Choice in Education, the Campaign for Real Education, and Parents for English Education.
Between them, and with increasing frequency as the 1980s progressed,
these groups or their members published articles and pamphlets (Honeyford, 1982, 1983, 1984, 1987; Hastie, 1984; Flew, 1984; Hillgate Group,
1986, 1987); four books: (Palmer 1986; O'Keeffe, 1986; Honeyford,
1988; Naylor, 1989) and actively supported parents opposed in various
ways to 'multicultural' education (see Naylor, 1989).

Despite the plethora of titles, Gordon (1986, 1989) argues that the
groups had an overlapping small core of members (comprising, in particular, Baroness Cox, Nicolas Seaton, Roger Scruton, Fred Naylor, John
Marks and Stuart Sexton). Gordon and others (eg Hill, 1990) argue that
they were extremely influential, partly through the strategy of creating a
multiplicity of organisations, and hence generating considerable 'noise'.
Their influence is also clearly to be seen in a selective media sensitisation
to issues of 'race'. They supported what became *cause celebrés* —
Honeyford in Bradford (see Foster-Carter in Troyna, 1987), the Dewsbury
parents who wanted their children sent to a school with fewer Asian pupils
(Naylor, 1989), and the parents in Cleveland who didn't want their
daughter to go to a school where they sang nursery rhymes in a south
Asian language. Their publications have inveighed against world studies,
peace studies, educational theory in teacher training, as well as 'alien
multiculturalism'. They have had an effect in the construction of a 'debate'
about nationalism, and in the Education Reform Act itself, with its
'Christian' assemblies, its abolition of the ILEA, and its marginalisation
of 'race'-related measures. More latterly their influence may be seen in
the reduction in what became allowable under Section 11 funding.

The construction of a media agenda has been particularly effective.
Goldsmith's College Communications Group (1987) traced a series of
stories which emerged in the mid-1980s characterising some councils
(especially in London) as 'loony left'. This extended beyond education to
include the GLC and its leader, and at various times included the leaders
of Haringey and Brent too, and a whole range of alleged 'policies'. Black

bin liners were condemned as racist, teachers were not allowed to say 'blackboard', only 'non-white' coffee could be requested in GLC canteens, singers of 'baa baa black sheep' had to substitute green sheep.

The Goldsmith's study observes that of the ten stories they researched in detail,

> ... two ... proved to be wholly false. There was no event, order or instruction which could have possibly formed the basis for these stories (p.18).

Of the rest, one came to be 'true' because nursery workers believed press accounts of a ban, and the others proved to have some connection with some event or set of facts, but were so distorted as to be unrecognisable.

Not all national papers showed equal interest in these stories. The *Sun* is implicated in nine out of ten stories, and the *Daily Mail* in six out of ten. The *Daily Mail*'s sister papers, the *Mail on Sunday* and the London *Evening Standard*, are also prominent in a significant number of instances (p.19). The *Sun* is the subject of another study, indicating that its treatment of education is consistent in terms of politics and racism with its treatment of other issues (Searle, 1989).

They go on to comment on the dissemination of this fiction outside London where it first pupated:

> A worrying feature of much of the press coverage is that many of the stories are lifted from the national press or from news agency releases and are reproduced uncritically in the regional press... The journalists on these papers cannot easily check the facts of these stories, and a wholly misleading impression is consequently given to people living outside the capital (1987, p.19).

This was aptly demonstrated at the 1987 NAME conference in Chichester. One of the keynote speakers, then leader of Brent, referred ironically to the 'Baa baa black sheep ban'. Despite having a printed copy of her speech, a local reporter assumed he 'knew' about this affair and reported her as defending the mythical ban (Gaine and Pearce, 1988).

In 1989 I asked five groups of students in Sussex, comprising teachers on an in-service course, primary and secondary BEds and PGCEs, about these stories. On average 30% could tell me confidently in which London LEAs they 'occurred', and many insistently added others they 'knew' about. 'Memories' of these 'events' are still easily stirred in student groups in 1994, with a new term to mock: 'political correctness'.

The individuals and the 'policies' became folk devils, easy touchstones against which people could interpret, trivialise and discount egalitarian measures. The agenda having been set, new stories simply had to press the right buttons to evoke a renewed reaction. In 1988 a single copy of an ILEA booklet about stereotyping in maths materials in a Wiltshire teachers' centre provoked national coverage in the *Sun, Daily Mail* and *Sunday Telegraph*. The terms 'loony left' and 'extremists' were employed, and interestingly, the 'information' was initially supplied to the *Daily Mail* by Fred Naylor, a Wiltshire county councillor and activist in several of the right-wing organisations mentioned above.

Another crucial episode was the labelling of Section 11 staff of the Brent Development Programme for Racial Equality as 'race spies'.

Race Spies Shock
Race Commissars in a left-wing borough are recruiting 180 Thought Police to patrol schools for prejudice. And they will be paid for out of a £5 million Government grant intended to promote racial harmony. But teachers in the London borough of Brent — who say they already work in a climate of fear — believe the classroom spies will cause lasting damage in the drive for equality and will lower education standards even further. Government ministers, who are powerless to prevent taxpayers' money being used, are worried that it could rapidly be copied by other inner-city councils.

The story was first mounted by the *Mail on Sunday* in October 1986, and although Brent's was a Section 11 scheme and hence agreed by theHome Office and the DES, the Secretary of State appeared on TV the next day and confessed himself 'disturbed' and called for reports. An HMI inspection which was due in any case was presented as a special 'flying squad' and reported in record time, publishing (without a precedent) before the LEA had seen even a draft (Amory, 1987).

There were many criticisms of Brent in the Report, but not about their equality policies. The HMI said:

There is little evidence that the work is being distorted by improper practices to do with antisexist or antiracist policies...

53

...the response to ethnic and cultural diversity had been sensitive and helpful...

Antiracist policies had made:

...only modest inroads, but where progress was marked, had a beneficial effect (DES, 1987).

The inspectors also reported that the ethnic minority parents in the south of the borough felt that the antiracist policies had not gone far enough.

Baker, however, as Secretary of State called it 'the most disturbing report I have ever read...' and the press, especially the tabloids, greeted the report with 'The worst schools in Britain' and 'Flushing out the fanatics (*Express*); 'Good and bad side of 'loony' schools' (*Today*); 'Schools lashing for left' (*Sun*); 'Baker fury at Brent schools report' (*Star*); and 'These blackboard bunglers of Brent' (*Mail*). Another report was commissioned by Brent, chaired by Sir David Lane, former Conservative MP and former Chair of the Commission for Racial Equality, and yet another was sent by the DES under Baroness Cox, member of the Hillgate Group. Neither of these found evidence of bad educational practice in the DPRE, or any justification for the term 'race spies'.

Section 11 has been for 25 years an increasing source of support money for LEAs seeking to meet the needs of black pupils. Though often misused by LEAs claiming and then redirecting the funds, it has nevertheless been the primary source of bilingual, ESL, and antiracist work. In the summer of 1990 a review into Section 11 was concluded, announcing that only ESL work would be funded in future. (DES, 1990) (Two years later it was further announced that the projects and posts set up under this review would only be funded at 50% rather than the 75% level which had been provided since 1967.) In September 1990 the then Conservative Brent council announced the abolition of the DPRE. (At the same time it abolished the post of Chief Inspector, making the post-holder redundant. He was Robin Richardson, the architect of the innovative antiracist policy Berkshire adopted in 1983.)

A final example of the national climate about 'race' and education which had developed by the late 1980s is the report on Burnage High School, Manchester. In September 1986 a Bangladeshi boy was stabbed to death by a white fellow pupil. The Education Authority funded an enquiry into the death, led by a barrister and staffed by three black

54

educationalists of national standing. By early 1988 the Committee was ready to publish but could not obtain the consent of Manchester Metropolitan Council. A local newspaper obtained a copy of the recommendations, which it published, and the national press took up the story from there.

The report is over 500 pages long and the *Manchester Evening News* published only the final chapter. Nevertheless they did so with little editorial comment except for commendations for the thoroughness of the document. The enquiry came to 146 closely argued and researched conclusions, one of which was that though the murder was not racialist, it took place in a racist context.

> We have no doubt at all that the murder by Darren Coulbourn was not racialist. There is no evidence that he stabbed Ahmad Ullah because he was Asian or because he was looking for a 'Paki' to kill. This was not that sort of case at all.

They also said:

> ... it was a racist murder in the light of the culture and context in which it took place. Racism was one of the vital ingredients that brought these two boys together in that fatal encounter (MacDonald et al, 1989 p.45).

In the final summary they make several criticisms of the LEA, the head and the school in their handling of the antecedents and consequences of the murder itself. About 12 of these criticisms are about the concept of antiracism employed at the school, which the Enquiry called 'symbolic' or 'moral' antiracism'.

> Racism is ... placed in some kind of moral vacuum and is totally divorced from the more complex reality of human relations in the classroom, playground, or community (ibid, p.402).

> We do not believe that an effective antiracist policy can exist unless the other issues are also addressed and dealt with, in particular class and gender (ibid, p.348).

Amongst their detailed and subtle analyses they say that 'In practice, moral antiracism has been an unmitigated disaster' (p.402), by which they mean it focused solely on 'race', it did not make connections between class and gender, so it failed to engage with the lived experience of the largely working class white pupils in this all-boys school. It was because of this inadequate overall perspective, the enquiry argued, that things had gone wrong. It was not antiracism which was the problem but a form of antiracism which was insufficiently aware of other social inequalities, a form of antiracism which was not left-wing enough.

The conspiracy theorists like Flew and the CPS could have found in this report confirmation that antiracism was merely a Trojan horse of the Left; instead they joined the national press in a much cruder stance: the murder had been caused by antiracist policies and should serve as a warning to those with 'left-wing' ideas.

> They proceeded to mount a sustained attack on antiracism, antiracist policies, 'looney-left' Councils with such policies, and antiracist approaches in education and schools. 'Burnage' was suddenly writ large as a question mark against antiracist education.
>
> A number of education officers who for years had resisted any notions of multi-culturalism let alone antiracism ... considered their position vindicated. Here, at last, was official endorsement of their view that antiracism was dangerous... It had even 'led to a killing' (Macdonald *et al*, 1989, p.xix-xxi).

The outcome in the Education Reform Act and in education policy

The agenda set in the media evidently had real political effects. This can be hard to quantify, though it clearly had its part to play in Brent. Berkshire's policy, too, was nearly abolished by its Conservative council in 1988 (Gaine, 1988; Tomlinson, 1990). Reference to 'hard-line', 'inter-fering' or 'ideological' LEAs peppered the debate about the abolition of the ILEA. Other effects have been the 'need' for a national curriculum, the diminunition of LEA powers inherent in LMS and grant maintained schools, and the possible demise of LEAs altogether with the centralisa-tion of teachers' pay and county reorganisation. At the Conservative conference in 1987, referring to the measures to be included in the ERA a year later, Thatcher said:

In the inner cities where youngsters must have a decent education if they are to have a better future, that opportunity is all too often snatched from them by hard-left education authorities and extremist teachers. Children who need to be able to count and multiply are learning antiracist mathematics, whatever that may be'

Tomlinson comments:

Overall, opposition to multicultural and antiracist curriculum developments slowly became, during the 1980s, a recognisable right-wing political tool for encouraging a populist view that any such developments threatened traditional education. With this kind of opposition it was not surprising that curriculum reformers have found difficulty in persuading colleagues, councillors, parents and others that multicultural and antiracist aims and activities were in fact directed towards the creation of a more just, decent and humane education system (1990, p.93).

The right-wing 'think tanks' and pressure groups became steadily more influential towards the end of the decade. The Parental Alliance for Choice in Education had one of its Council appointed to the National Curriculum working group on mathematics. By 1987 Hempel reported that PACE and the Campaign for Real Education were meeting regularly at the House of Lords, the meetings being chaired by Baroness Cox, who in 1988 was a key figure in shaping the RE provisions of the Education Act, as well as being a Council member of the CNAA. Other avowed Thatcher supporters aside, the NCC gained a member of the Centre for Policy Studies: John McIntosh. SEAC gained another of their members, Dr John Marks (also of the Hillgate Group).

At their 1990 conference, the Campaign for Real Education (by then numbering Ray Honeyford amongst its prominent supporters) felt able to claim to have played a significant role in bringing about the Education Reform Act, a claim reinforced by Davies, Holland and Minhas (1990) in a critical paper about one of the Campaign's right-wing stablemates

The Hillgate Group portray antiracism as an assault on British values and since they have been the chief architects of the 1988 Education Reform Act they see the National Curriculum as a countermeasure against equal opportunity policies (p.25).

In the autumn of 1990 the CPS published a pamphlet on teacher training, continuing a theme first elaborated by the Social Affairs Unit in *The Wayward Curriculum* (O'Keeffe, 1986). In it Sheila Lawlor, Deputy Director of the CPS, argued that teacher training had been captured by a leftish establishment who dwelt on theory and the interminable analysis of inequality rather than practical classroom skills. Despite injunctions from the Conservative-created Committee for the Accreditation of Teacher Education (CATE: 1984; 1989) that students must be encouraged to 'guard against preconceptions based on race' the notion that the antiracist folk devils have taken over teacher training is, as Hill (1990) argues, part of a more general assault by the Right on egalitarian practices in education.

By the time 1990 came to an end, the explicit placing of members of right-wing pressure groups and think tanks was well established. New ministerial appointments to CATE (including Anthony O'Hear, member of several such think tanks) were being referred to as 'stiffening' by the TES, Lawlor's husband was made the chair of SEAC's English Committee, and so it went on. By 1993 the Conservative chair of the Commons Select Committee on Education had openly complained that Tory Education policy was in the hands of a right-wing clique, a point echoed ruefully by the former chair of the NCC English Committee, originally a Baker-Thatcher appointee (Cox: 1993).

Education policy-making was transformed in the Thatcher-Major era. Previously, it had been decentralised and, at best,the outcome of debate or conflict between the key players of teacher unions, LEAs, government, HMI, and individual schools (and at worst a muddle). Increasingly, the tone of non-consultation set by Baker in 1988 was developed into a speciality by Clarke and then Patten, who gave increasing powers to themselves and future Secretaries of State in a series of Education Acts distinguished mostly by being hasty, long and ragbags of disconnected provisions. The curriculum is now determined centrally, as are the ways, times and fine details of how it will be assessed. The content and indeed philosophy of teacher education is increasingly strictly controlled. LEAs can make policies but have few funds to put behind them. Schools almost dare not be innovative, or be perceived as 'radical' because of the marketing philosophy inherent in local financial management.

In later chapters I shall explore what spaces and opportunities this leaves for antiracist work, especially in white schools. In brief, it is clear that the scope for teacher, school and LEA action is less than it was a decade ago and that as regards antiracism this is an intentional outcome of the broader educational project of the Right.

Chapter 4

Teaching about 'race' and racism

> Political education should, through encouraging pupils to consider how power is exercised and by whom at different levels in our society, how resources are allocated, how policies are determined and implemented, how decisions are taken and how conflicts are resolved, be no more likely to lead them to question and challenge the status quo, other than where this is justified, than to defend and seek to retain it (Swann Report, 1985, p.334).

There is an increasing number of classroom books, materials and teaching packs with a multicultural focus (see Sources), but there are fewer which deal directly with 'race' and racism. This is understandable — there is more nervousness about it on the part of almost everyone and it is undoubtedly difficult to tackle (though teachers do harder things). This chapter explores some of the difficulties. There is more of an emphasis on the secondary phase in part of the argument (about assessment and public exams), but this should not be taken to mean that it is a secondary preserve: there are enough examples in chapter one to demonstrate that the notion of 'childhood innocence' is sometimes wishful thinking.

It is one thing to complain that pupils believe a web of pernicious myths about black and Asian people, but quite another to translate this complaint into action in the form of classroom practice. Though few in number, there are now several practical accounts of curriculum initiatives in largely white schools, both primary and secondary. Such accounts not only warn us of pitfalls, they show the rewards and possibilities of making the necessary efforts, and certainly a strong example of effective curriculum work is a powerful persuader of doubtful colleagues.

A detailed primary example is Epstein's *Changing Classroom Cultures* (1993). This has Epstein herself as the key figure, in one case as head teacher and in the other as advisory teacher, and contains detailed accounts of how particular changes were brought about, warts and all. There are also stimulating discussions about pedagogy (how can we teach about oppression without democratising classrooms?) child-centredness (are not primary pupils too young for these things?) and micro-politics (how does opposition and support show itself in the co-operative world of the primary school?).

Grudgeon and Woods (1990) defy antiracist strictures about the naiveness of presenting the whole issue as a positive curriculum opportunity and do just that in two of their accounts. One is of a school exchange between a white rural school and a multiracial city one, another is of a small church school pursuing a particular theme (living and growing) with a 'multicultural' perspective. The accounts are brief and the researchers make only modest claims about the success of the work described, but key issues are discussed: conceptions of teaching; the trap of exoticising some 'other cultures' (clearly fallen into by one school); the use of reference materials; the teachers' examination (or not) of their own assumptions; the dependence on the personal commitment and energy of key people. (See Brown et al, 1990, for a reflective and practical guide to twinning).

Carrington and Short (1989) contains two case studies of work in all-white primary schools, one in a 'respectable' working class area, the other in a social priority area. The interesting thing about these studies is that, unlike Grudgeon and Woods they focus on the awareness of racism and inequality (of various kinds) amongst the 11-12 year olds and explicitly engaging with it. They combine the use of factual material, creative writing and a novel (*The Trouble with Donovan Croft* by Ashley, 1975) to promote discussion in the class about 'race', all as part of a wider project on changes in life-styles since the war.

Other accounts of how specific largely white schools have sought to raise 'race' on their curriculum agenda can be found in one chapter in Chivers (1987). Claire, Maybin and Swann (1993) also have two such chapters on work in primary schools, one about Native Americans, the other about travellers. Numerous others can be found in past editions of the journal *Multicultural Teaching*.

One of the most challenging accounts of someone's own practice is a reflective piece by Cohen in Donald and Rattansi (1992), about several years of antiracist youth work with potential (male) National Front members in a south London council estate. It is intricate in its analysis of 'narratives' of racism and antiracism running through teachers' theories and positions, arguing that we position ourselves as active in a story of continuing progress

> The onward march of reason and tolerance is led by the 'natural' standard bearers, the European intelligensia, and its various allies, who wage an unremitting battle against the irrational prejudices of both masses and traditional elites (p.71).

This almost inevitably endows us with a teacher's knowing stance against the 'cultural dopes', the pupils we teach, privileging our own role 'as guardians of reason and enlightenment,' in combating racism (p.72). Cohen suggests a more subtle way of 'reading' the comments and arguments of young racists, locating their comments in the contexts in which they are uttered (like school) and the ways in which they are built up in their daily lives. A key point Cohen makes is that this is not 'old racism' in the sense of a single and relatively simple logic of biological (or even cultural) superiority/inferiority. There is not a self-confident overall theory in what the boys say, but a series of accounts, stories and explanations

> ... which resort to all manner of rhetorical devices to construct a narrative of special pleading marked by highly ambiguous and ironic self-reference and a litany of real or imagined grievance (p.93).

It is this, Cohen argues, with which we must engage, rather than our own interpretive gloss on what young people are saying: 'They just need the right information'; 'they get it from their parents'; 'working class culture is racist'; 'the capitalist press peddle all this' and so on.

In the 1980s I and a colleague tried to address some of the problems of teaching about 'race' via a term's work as part of a social studies/sociology examined course, recounted in detail in Gaine (1987). I only want to extract a few key details here and, along with the studies mentioned above, consider the dilemmas and issues involved. But first, a quotation from Sue, aged 15. She was not entirely typical but is nonetheless indicative of needs, hopes and possibilities. The quotation is a series of reactions to the course we devised, beginning with a simulation called 'Passport', in which she has been given the role of an Indian trying to enter Britain in the 1960s and get around the discrimination she meets:

> When I first walked in I didn't know what to expect, just a sort of play or something. When they first gave out the envelopes and things I thought it was a bit stupid and didn't really see the point of it. At first, when we started playing, I thought it was a big joke, but then, trying to get my pretend wife over and trying to get a job, I began to get a bit impatient and angry because no-one would help us. Every time we wanted something there was always an excuse to stop me, people kept calling me Paki as if colour mattered, and that made me feel angry, not just at them but at myself, 'cos I've done the same sort of thing, not out loud but to myself as I saw a coloured person. The things the people in the drama thing wanted to know had no relevance to me, I didn't realise that that sort of thing actually goes on. I know it was acting and everything was overdone, but if I got angry and annoyed during that short time, only 45 minutes, I wonder how the coloured people feel going through it every minute in every day, it must be humiliating and degrading.

> When my pretend wife said 'Go over and get a job and send me back the money', I didn't want to leave her, and I didn't want to be on my own, where I didn't know anybody. Then I worked as hard as I could to get the money and then we had to fill in a form, then another form. In the end we bribed the man to let us through... The next time I see a coloured person I expect I'll pity them, but I don't expect they want pity either, I won't know what to do or say, but I will pity them inside. I'm really glad I'm not coloured, not because of the colour but because of what they have to go through just in order to live a life, and even that life isn't really pleasant.

Coloured people are always called names like wogs, Pakis, jungle bunnies etc. I don't even understand these names yet I use them.

White people seem so false and hypocritical to the black people. Coloured people seem so down to earth and real. From watching the film I know people hurt, but I never knew how much they hurt. I didn't realise some things went on. I wish I hadn't been brought up in a racist culture then maybe I wouldn't feel so guilty now. When you read things in the paper about fights and things involving black people you don't think about the white people involved and you think 'Oh, that doesn't involve me so why should I worry'.

I wish I knew a coloured person, I mean, really well, then if I went out with them I could feel I wasn't racist and I didn't care, but that's hypocritical as well, because I would know their colour and I shouldn't care about it.

I would like to write to a coloured person in another school in Britain... but wouldn't the person mind being singled out to write to me just because they are coloured?... Maybe it will make me feel and react better if I know just how they feel about everything... we think they owe us a lot, but really the way most of them are treated they don't owe us nothing but hate... (Sue, aged 15).

The problem of curriculum space

In trying to examine racism in class, one central problem is finding the time to do it well. It seldom gets much time or space in school, and committed and concerned teachers wonder about raising it because they doubt their skill and fear lest they, if not create a problem where none existed, perhaps make it worse. 'Stirring the pot' for half an hour, without the time either then or later to help the contents settle in a way which would be positive educationally, can certainly make things worse. It has the effect of raising a vague background problem in many pupils' minds and bringing it forward, without enabling any resolution to take place. As many teachers will know, what happens next is an eruption of opinion and argument, a dozen separate sub-issues about 'race' spring up (typically Chinese takeaways, religion, crash helmets, immigration, mugging, riots, unemployment, social security, and the smell of curry). The issue of 'race' is like an octopus, hack off one tentacle and the others grab hold of you; worry the thing too much and it squirts ink everywhere.

None can be adequately addressed and the class tumbles out when the bell goes, to a mixture of relief and despair on the part of the teacher. She has met the octopus. What can s/he do? Where to start? Where did she go wrong? Has she made it worse?

Indeed she has, but it is hardly her fault. The class jokers have had their role reinforced and they exchange racist jokes for the rest of the morning; the majority of pupils, who will have had a mixture of confusions, half truths, anecdotes, and strong feelings about 'race' in the first place, will have these agitated a little; the (rare) pupil who stands outside this common pattern will be able to find no other role but silence; and if there is a black or Asian child in the class s/he will just have to be angry all day, or helplessly join in the 'joking', or emotionally withdraw, and in any case will wish that Miss had got on with the proper lesson: 'Things were all right until you started talking about it'.

None of this is a justification for doing nothing, but it does highlight the complexity of the issue and the difficulty of brief interventions: you cannot cover 'prejudice' in an hour. By the time they get to secondary school many pupils already have a good deal to unlearn about 'race'. To unlearn it requires building up a good deal of trust, a consistent engagement with the routinely recited racism of pupils (learned in part through their peer group) and a careful insistence on respect for evidence.

Academic or pastoral?

In the 1990s, by far the most likely 'home' of any teaching about racism is in the secondary pastoral curriculum. In some ways this is clearly where it belongs — after all, we are dealing in large part with attitudes, values and aspects of citizenship. But racism has to fight for space in this curriculum slot with many other concerns, (conceivably everything from personal hygiene and greeting visitors on the one hand to aspects of RE, sex, health, drugs and careers on the other: HMI *Curriculum Matters* 14; 1989). Of course, a great many issues press for curriculum time and space and it is hard to argue that this one is more important than all the others, but it is crucial to underline that any brief course or module is likely merely to scratch the surface.

One of the reasons my colleague and I chose the mainstream/examined route in the 1980s was to avoid this dangerous superficiality. Another was more to do with our objectives. There is a clear and necessary focus in much PSE work on discussion, listening to others' opinions, agreeing to differ and examining values. While these are necessary skills to develop in examining racism, there are others, perhaps more often associated with 'worthwhile' activities elsewhere in the curriculum. We assessed pupils according to the exam board's four criteria of:

1. Knowledge;

2. The ability to locate and select evidence;

3. The interpretation of evidence and evaluation of argument;

4. The presentation of explanations, ideas and arguments.

These were weighted so that the first counted for more than each of the others, and assessment tasks had to be set so they tested these skills.

The point here is that in principle a good deal of the work we did could be assessed in much the same way as other subjects. Studying racism does not have to be mostly a matter of 'discussions', attitudes and feelings, and so best dealt with as a matter of opinions. People's feelings cloud and shape the issues but there are nevertheless facts and evidence, historical, cultural and economic analyses, media biases and geographical distributions, all of which are employed in studying wars, industrial decline, smoking, and many other things which have a toe-hold in the mainstream curriculum. If we value academic skills we ought to be prepared to apply them to the sharp end of teaching and learning, and to develop skills of evidence and judgement, separating emotive from factual statements, as well as all the skills of reading, studying, and appropriate language use which schools are rightly expected to impart. None of this is particularly easy. Assessing such work is difficult because of the complexity of learning about 'race', but the difficulty has to be welcomed since it gets to grips with something which matters in education.

We used a sociology/social studies course with 'race' as a large element in it, set up in a school where for various reasons the circumstances were favourable to this strategy. In principle, the case for such a discrete, separate, formally assessed course about racism can still be made. However, specific changes in the school in question effectively brought the course to an end, and the extent of prescription in the National Curriculum (to say nothing of some politicians' distaste for sociology) have caused a reduction in the numbers doing sociology at 16+ compared with its hitherto expanding numbers. In practice, therefore, difficult though it was to get such a course established in the mid-eighties, it has been very much harder since. In any case, we are to some extent discussing fire brigade tactics here: we ought to aim at a situation where the efforts of primary schools and a concerted approach in secondary school means that pupils do not have such a lot to unlearn.

A more recent case study in another subject area is provided by Naidoo (1992), who takes us through a year's work — mainly in English lessons — with a year 9 class in an all-white school. It was a focused attempt to chart the problems and effects of teaching about racism through literature, and the book is probably the most detailed available about the day to day events, reactions, decisions and dilemmas she encountered, some involving staff, some involving individual and group dynamics with students. She discusses the books she used: her own *Journey to Jo'burg* — though at the time the pupils did not know she was the author; *Buddy* by Nigel Hinton (1983); *Friedrich* (Richter, 1961/1978); *Roll of Thunder, Hear my Cry* (Taylor, 1987) and *Waiting for the Rain* (Gordon, 1987). There was also a good deal of drama and 'hotseating', visits by a range of people from outside the school: a black poet, a race relations worker, others in role, some involvement from RE using the BBC series 'Getting to Grips with Racism', a visit to the Anne Frank Exhibition, and some taught input about the ideology of 'race'. The book is clearly of great value to any English teacher interested in this kind of work but also has the feel of real classrooms about it and points up many of the issues which arise when 'race' comes up in secondary lessons. There are accounts from pupils, transcripts of their reactions, and the author's reflections on the pupils who underwent a positive shift in attitudes and a couple who, arguably, were reinforced in their initial racism.

Status

Another argument for trying to locate such work in the 'mainstream' or examined curriculum is about status, though making such a case is fraught with difficulty. Many teachers (to say nothing of pupils) believe that the secondary curriculum is too dominated by public examinations and that some erosion of this might allow more 'real' education to take place. One way of eroding the space taken by exam work is obviously to build up the non-examined curriculum and simultaneously break the stranglehold of educational labelling. But idealists in one field often see themselves as realists in another and, as far as public exams (broadly defined) are concerned, it seems to me realistic to expect their continued domination of secondary education and no decline in society's expectation that schools will have a grading function. If this is the case then the important work of a school will continue to be seen as the assessment-orientated work, so if 'race' is important it should be included with the other things schools give priority to. After all, what kind of argument is it which, in effect, does not question the divine right of geography and German to remain as examinable subjects, while newer concerns have to fight the double battle of recognition and of status. (The battle has to be fought in pupils' minds too; they have little doubt about what 'counts' in school.)

Other issues and problems

'Bias'

Any teacher involved in this kind of work runs the risk of simplistic charges of bias, however much they might insist that their real purpose was more to do with encouraging a critical awareness than with imposing a single interpretation or account. This is even more of a danger when formally assessed work is involved and pupils' racism or antiracism is (allegedly) being marked (especially if teachers fall too neatly into the trap described by Cohen). There are undoubted problems when pupils' emotions get in the way of their factual judgements, and many would argue that the same is true of teachers. On the other hand, I have little time for the standpoint of pretending not to have a standpoint, nor for the 'objectivity' which leads so many white people to disbelieve what black and Asian people tell them.

69

I can offer no simple solution to these problems. My own way of dealing with them was always to give them the classroom time they need, which means a willingness to converse at length with the pupils involved in a way which allows them to speak, think aloud and not feel put down. Sharing the problem with other staff at various levels and with parents, can also prevent simplistic charges of bias suddenly arising. They will still arise from time to time, but to seek to eschew affective and political dimensions in 'academic' subjects is take the road to irrelevance. A curriculum in which the things that count in people's lives are consigned to 'pastoral' and things that are drained of everyday relevance are examined would be a fundamentally misguided one.

Teacher skill

Skills are another issue in pastoral programmes, though in a way this is a by-product of time constraints. In schools so organised that a small team of staff do most of the pastoral 'lessons', expertise can build up. Like many things in teaching, teaching about 'race' is a matter of technique, but there is no particular reason to expect teachers of all subject backgrounds to have the knowledge and skills to handle such a tricky topic confidently. Indeed, they would be right to be wary of jumping into deep water with this particular octopus. It is worth saying that wherever and whenever racism is tackled in the curriculum it needs courage, and that sometimes means the courage to make mistakes. This needs practice.

Monitoring and responding to pupils' feelings

Despite the emphasis above on the traditional trappings of secondary school work, the importance of the affective dimension should not be forgotten. This is a recurring theme in Naidoo's book (and in a way in Cohen's and Epstein's accounts), emerging quite explicitly in drama and where pupils adopted the roles of various characters in the books they studied.

There is a very detailed account of one approach to monitoring how pupils are feeling in chapters 3 and 4 of *No Problem Here* (Gaine, 1987) with lengthy transcripts of pupils' writing, so it is not necessary to repeat it here. Suffice it to say that in that case study, pupils were encouraged to write a personal log after each lesson of a term's course, to which the teacher replied in written notes.

The logs were an attempt to be aware of the 'informal' processes of learning which intertwine with the usual formal appearances. They asked pupils to reflect, in an organised but informal way, on what they have learned or not learned, allowing the teacher to participate in this reflection too. With classes of thirty or more it is impossible in even the most apparently straightforward lesson to be aware of what many of the class are getting out of it. Any good teacher knows how misleading it is to generalise from the pupils who talk the most or from written work which is directly assessed. Yet the teacher needed to monitor pupils' responses in some way in order to avoid teacher domination of the acceptable things to express, and to stay in touch with pupils' feelings and reactions, and their needs from the lesson. These logs, therefore, were an attempt to get pupils to write a few of their thoughts, to aid their own sense of direction in learning but also to give the teacher some idea of the way their views differed from hers about what was happening.

Worthwhile though they are, such logs take a large amount of teacher time on top of the more formal marking load generated by the course, which was enormous. To use learning logs as well was extra workload. Of course, it makes one's understanding of the class better and therefore one's teaching ought to be better, but it still takes some of that most scarce of good teachers' possessions, time. It has to be confessed, therefore, that it is a very idealistic recommendation.

Using pupils' feelings

Problems about assessment and about pupils' feelings interfering with 'rational' judgement have already been touched upon. We can, however, also learn through our feelings. 'Race' carries an emotional charge, and to experience something of the feelings of others can be a powerful means of learning. Affective literature and emotive films aside, the most obvious tool for a teacher wanting to bring about this kind of learning is simulation: it ought to be used, with all its difficulties. In the 'Passport' game mentioned earlier, feelings can run high and there can be some physical pushing and shoving, though I have never had anyone actually come to blows. Some people may withdraw and sit it out because it has become too much for them, some may get close to tears with frustration. Obviously this has to be handled in a context which the pupils know to be caring, but I have few reservations about using such a potentially dramatic technique. 'Race' evokes strong feelings for many white (and black and Asian) people, and I know of no other technique which gives a flavour of what discrimination feels like for its targets. The fact that it hurts is one of the things that has to be put over, and although it may be controversial and explosive, we are scarcely really touching the issue unless we grasp the nettles involved. One of them is pupils' feelings.

An effective substitute for actually doing a simulation is the film 'A Class Divided', where two very powerful simulations are shown. There are passages where the feelings of those experiencing discrimination fill the screen and most viewers cannot help but identify with them (more details on p.113).

Victimology

Another potential criticism of this kind of work is that it can present black and Asian people in Britain as helpless victims, always poor, 'disadvantaged', a pitiable stereotype. The real effort needed to avoid this in largely white areas should not be underestimated (nor, perhaps, should mistakes be too harshly judged).

There is an apparent paradox in this aspect of antiracist work: our aim is for 'race' to be irrelevant, for people not to be categorised by something like skin colour but to receive equal treatment as individuals. Yet to achieve this we have first to recognise that, in practice, 'race' *is* relevant and to understand how racism works. Thus those most concerned to end racism are also the most concerned to identify it. Identification can require, at times or at first, regarding the group an individual belongs to as more significant than many of her or his other qualities and attributes. In dealing with 'race' as a key determinant in people's life chances, in recognising that it is a key category in British society, some stereotyping, some over-simple portrayal, is probably inevitable. It is not possible for every pupil (or teacher) to know real black and Asian people against whom to check their generalisations. In beginning to learn about groups who have different experiences of oppression from ourselves, especially those of whom we have no first-hand experience, it may sometimes be necessary to see them as 'categories' first before developing more subtle understandings of how resistance, individuality and ordinary human lives coexist with oppression. We do not have to stop at such a portrayal of simple categories (black people; 'the disabled'; Muslims; unemployed youth; lesbians) but any understanding of structural patterns may need to start with such portrayals.

A partial answer to this problem is for pupils to meet and talk with black and Asian visitors and speakers, but this is not always possible — there are not enough black and Asian people to go round. Another partial answer is the use of video and audio material, of which a good deal has been produced over the past decade (some examples are on pp.112-113). These allow black and Asian people to speak for themselves rather than to be represented by books, statistics, or white teachers, though there is no easy answer to the question of which black and Asian people are chosen to 'speak' either in the flesh or on film. A third, related, strategy is to use fiction, which can make the link between individual lives and wider social processes without either apolitical individualism or simplistic determinism. Finally, and more often possible in primary schools where cross-curricular work is easier, there are the exchanges and letters made possible in twinning multiracial and all-white schools (see Brown et al; 1989).

Isolated black and Asian pupils

In many 'white' schools there is a single black or Asian pupil in the class, or a very small number. Ideally, a teacher knows such pupils and has their trust before exposing them to a classroom focus on racism. Preferably, the teacher has talked to the pupil and her/his parents beforehand. Their reactions will vary, of course, before, during and after any class work.

There are times when it is uncomfortable for a black or Asian pupil to be in the class. For instance, a single Chinese girl is at the back of a class who are discussing racist names. They agree about the offensiveness of 'Paki shop' but are not sure about 'Chinky takeaway'.

I suggest we need to err on the side of caution, that people probably do not like being referred to in that way and the Chinese girl nods vehemently (unseen by the rest of the class). Do I ask her directly so the class can see how she feels? She is telling me she hates the name, and the others need to know, but for her to tell them is also to tell them how to hurt her.... I have had occasions when black and Asian children have been upset enough to be in tears at the end of a lesson when the others have left, and at such times it is difficult to be unequivocally sure of what one is doing.

(With some classes, it is worth anticipating the worst and giving the solitary black or Asian pupil the option of working elsewhere. There ought to be support systems available so that adults or older pupils can give support to black or Asian pupils in this position, but this is easier said than done in the maelstrom of the average school.)

On the other hand, I have no reason to think that on balance my former black and Asian pupils wished the issue had been ignored. It is scary and it is easy to get it wrong, but it is contributing to a conspiracy of nervous silence not to try.

Words and names

At some stage terminology has to be discussed and agreed upon with a class. In the case of a word like 'Paki' it takes some pupils a while to recognise it as an insult. Often they seem to need a clearer idea of the geography of the sub-continent to appreciate that it is senseless to apply the term to all 'Asians', and then they need some empathy to grasp that it is more than a simple abbreviation even when only applied to Pakistanis. Even then, they still have to care enough to bother not to use insulting terms, including the more obvious ones.

If all else fails I fall back on teacher authority: I would find frequent use of such terms in my classroom too offensive to tolerate. It is a matter of regret if pupils are unwilling to accept this, but in the last analysis teachers have to consider the black and Asian children, potential or actual, in the school, and they have a right to expect that powerfully insulting terms of abuse are not acceptable currency. I also think that adult modelling matters, and that to an extent using either racist or non-racist terminology is habit-forming.

The use of the term 'black' is rather more subtle, however, and while there is a strong argument for its use in relation to some people, it cannot be quickly presented to the average year 10 class (let alone anyone younger) who, in largely white areas, tend to think of it as offensive and to prefer 'coloured'. As a first step one can get pupils to word-associate on 'black', perhaps having previously prepared a list from a dictionary of the terms, almost all negative, which include the word. The point is to start pupils thinking about their own resistance to the word and the subtlety of the attitudes involved. It is not a point which all pupils will write eloquent-

ly about, but two extracts from a year 8 class demonstrate that the point
can be made.

I never really thought about how it was the slaves that made us feel
superior. Then when we thought about all the words it seems funny
how so many mean so much about black people, so they've ended up
with a stereotype.

We wrote and discussed images and information about black people
and all these images are negative. Having all negative images of a
person or race is not a good thing as it encourages others to be negative
as well. If we gradually introduced facts and images about black
people that are positive then perhaps people's ideas of these people
would change.

A simplistic view of culture?

Any study of racism in a largely white area needs to involve some
informational, factual element about Britain's Asian and black population.
This is not tokenist multiculturalism: it is clearing away some myths,
half-truths and ignorance. Racism is not caused by ignorance but it feeds
on it, so pupils ought to know that Bangladesh is not in India and that the
idea of British culture cannot be understood without reference to the
Caribbean (why are Jamaica's three counties called Cornwall, Surrey and
Middlesex?) They also need some inoculation against Islamaphobia.
(They may not want to know, of course. Sometimes pupils do not listen
to the distinctions between Sikhs and Muslims, or even West Indians and
Indians, because they already believe that these people are responsible for
Britain's unemployment, bad housing, crime and national decline. Why
should they care about the differences among the peoples allegedly
responsible for all our ills?)

It is not easy to teach about culture in a very few lessons without being
oversimplistic and patronising. It is probably impossible, and black and
Asian people living in areas where they can expect at least some white
people to be respectfully conscious of their cultures will be appalled at
the digest offered to many white children in their name. In a way I am not
sure there is any alternative, since however long it is any digest will seem
like a 'Cook's tour' to someone better informed. 'Bringing in an ethnic
minority person' does not solve the problem either, since even if there

were enough people available during the day, they might not want to go into everyone's classroom as walking cultural curios, or feel able to condense 'Bengali culture' into 40 minutes.

The trouble is there is no such thing as 'Caribbean' or 'Asian' culture; they are not static, simple or solid entities. The harder one looks for them the clearer three things become. First, there are many differences within the broader headings. Thus, in certain company it is offensive to speak of 'Asians' because Gujeratis, or Panjabi Sikhs, or Sylhetis would be far better descriptions, just as 'European' is seldom a usefully precise label for anyone. Similarly, Trinidadians tire of the assumption that all African-Caribbeans are Jamaican (so do Jamaicans). Second, how does one choose a particular cultural feature as an important one, and who chooses? This leads to a third realisation: it is difficult to make many generalisations without being racist.

Even with an apparently homogeneous group, cultural generalisations are suspect. The generalisations people make about the British are easily recognised as simplistic stereotypes, unless we believe them ourselves. In such cases they are usually favourable: *we* are inventive, defenders of freedom, appropriately reserved, patriotic, and animal loving. We are not debilitatingly nostalgic, over-hierarchical, or jingoistic, though others think we are. What, then, can we legitimately say about Pakistanis? They are likely to be Muslims to be sure, but as a group of British Pakistanis have said:

> Muslim piety is not exactly a myth, but it has certainly developed new dimensions under the flood of material about Islam as a religion, and the dearth of material about Muslims as human beings. We don't exactly take our religion for granted, but we can feel sufficiently comfortable in it to spend much of our time trying to earn our living, raise our status, and even enjoy ourselves. It is our duty to defend our religion as need arises, but we believe that many multicultural enthusiasts have been misled by the fanatical fringe that has fostered the religious theme to the exclusion of all else (1984).

Since that was written, Muslims have increasingly been identified as a specific sub-group within British Asians, and the term is often carelessly assumed to be synonymous with 'fundamentalist', with no distinctions made between Sunni and Shi'a; young and old; Bengali and Panjabi; Arab and South Asian. This stereotype was reinforced during the Rushdie Affair, which produced a strong sense of religious affront amongst most British Muslims, but this (arguably) had more to do with a complex web of economic disadvantage and what Modood (1990) calls 'beseiged conservatism' than with 'fundamentalism'.

If we have to exercise caution when generalising about religion, when at least some basic precepts are written down and some people formally agree to them, then all generalisations about a group's attitudes, abilities and tastes must be even more suspect. If it is said, however well meaningly, that Gujeratis have a good business sense, Indians are hard-working, that the Hong Kong Chinese 'make good restaurateurs', or that African-Caribbeans are 'easy going', one can by the same token say that the Irish really are thick, Jamaicans are lazy, Pakistanis are money grabbing, and of course the Jews are mean. This makes written materials on these themes especially difficult to write.

All such generalisations are not so tenuous, of course. One which could easily support itself with sound statistical evidence is that a high proportion of British Asian marriages are arranged. How does the presenter of 'other cultures' deal with this? (Actually, with older white pupils it can scarcely be avoided since they mostly find it intriguing.) There are many factual issues (the practice has no necessary connection with religion; is not always the gruesome forced business it can be sensationalised as; does not inevitably treat women as chattels; is more about the union of families than about romantic love; and is subject to variation and change in the sub-continent, related to class and urbanisation) but there is a key issue of perspective. We have to be non-judgmental and we have to model a cautious unwillingness to take a simple position, because for too long white people have almost never commented upon such things as equals. It may be a measure of the mess we are in, but the fact is that white people cannot make public judgements about the cultural patterns of black people or Asian people and expect to have them taken at face value.

Besides, such judgements are often an escape route from the discomfort of looking at racism. As one British Pakistani woman put it, 'Leave our men's sexism to us, you deal with racism, that's your problem'. Another wrote in letter to the *Guardian* in 1989 with reference to comments about sexism in Islam:

A swift appraisal of the terrifying oppression of Western women — whose labour is cheap outside the home and free inside it, whose bodies are commodities and sales incentives in the media, who have no respect if they work and no self-respect if they do not, and who are conditioned to go to extraordinary and painful lengths to make their bodies palatable for men — a swift appraisal shows that Western women are as oppressed (if more subtly) as their sisters in Islam.

Optimists might say that the time will come when enough trust exists for such issues to be explored together, but we should not expect too much too soon.

I would therefore argue that all one should be prepared to do as a teacher is to let some Asian people speak, either in person, on film, or in written sources. There are sources which do this in a way that makes possible the beginnings of an understanding for white pupils who are obviously light years away from the value system in which arranged marriages can take place. Contested and contradictory positions can also be put: as regards the position of women, the films 'Black by Popular Demand' and 'In Their Own Words' are useful to counter simplistic stereotypes. Other materials are listed under 'Sources'.

Will pupils be negative and hostile because it is 'school knowledge'?

There is clearly a risk that if the material is presented as the way nice people like teachers think, then many pupils will make their own decisions about what to do with it. To be effective educators with some young people we have to go beyond merely treating them as cultural dopes, and the Burnage Report underlines the dangers of a moralistic, doctrinaire anti-racism which treats all young white people as inherently racist. On the other hand, the accounts in Gaine (1987), Massey (1991) and Naidoo (1992) show that many secondary pupils in all-white areas are more than willing to have school knowledge which really does help understand and grapple with the world outside. Even so, these accounts need to be read in conjunction with Cohen's work (1991; 1992) with much more hard-nosed youngsters.

How political does all this get?

Bias was touched upon earlier, but earlier still came the quotation from Swann which opened this chapter. We cannot examine racism without being political with a small 'p' and sometimes with a big 'P'. Examining racism means at times being critical of our society and doing so in settings where it may be considered very radical to do so, where to challenge racism either makes one a crackpot Marxist or an eroder of Christian England and subverter of the National Curriculum. It is worth it though, because it is possible to make a difference.

Chapter 5

Changing Your School — Histories

This chapter is about antiracist policies in white (mostly secondary) schools, their usefulness, the reasons in principle for having them, the arguments that might persuade people to adopt them, and the possible strategy differences in this between 'black' and 'white' schools. It is also more generally about developing consciousness about racism in a school and initiating some change, however small.

The focus and value of a policy

It ought to be made clear at once what I think such a policy ought to be about. My starting point in chapter 1 was that the majority of white pupils have considerable levels of confusion, misunderstanding and hostility about 'race', and that it is the duty of schools to tackle this in all the ways open to them. (If they do not then we will continue to fail black, Asian and white pupils alike, and any attempts to locate the problem solely in inner-city areas will not succeed.) Thus any policy ought to set out to deal both with the manifestations of racism against black and Asian pupils (and this can be an issue even if there is only one black pupil in the school), and with the contribution the curriculum and ethos of the school can make

81

towards eroding pupils' racism and replacing it with something else. As the NCC put it:

> ... a commitment to providing equal opportunities to all pupils, and a recognition that preparation for life in a multicultural society is relevant for all pupils, should permeate every aspect of the curriculum (NCC, 1990).

The Swann report commented:

> We... see education as having a major role to play in countering the racism which still persists in Britain today and which we believe constitutes one of the chief obstacles to the realisation of a truly pluralist society ...we believe that the education system and teachers in particular are uniquely placed to influence the attitudes of all young people in a positive manner (DES, 1985, p.319).

To those who see this as a negative and therefore unhelpful way of posing the issue, it may be useful to restate one of the points of Chapter 3, namely that the failure to recognise the extent of white racism has bedevilled educational responses in multiracial areas (where there have been any responses at all), and that if the white areas are to avoid such a painfully slow evolution of their own responses they have to stop thinking that education about 'race' is education about immigrants.

This discussion of school policies has to be set in the context of the other chapters, and a distinction made between how points may be phrased here and how they may be phrased in the early stages of discussion in a particular school. My basic argument in a school would, in principle, be the same as that above. In other words there is no real option other than to define the issue as racism and to define the school's task as responding to it. This is a negative and threatening educational task to present to people, and could be opposed on the grounds that it is strategically better to present challenges as positive rather than negative — it always feels better to be creating a new world rather than reacting to the problems of the old one. Thus a broader and richer curriculum could be the carrot, and a more effective incentive than the stick of racism. This may, on occasion, be good strategy, but it should not be confused with our basic understanding of the problem. In fact, I am not convinced it is even good strategy, since my own experience has been that teachers do not really get to grips with a new 'multicultural' curriculum until they have recognised the racism of the old one, and the most effective way of showing the penetration of racism into their daily work is to show them what their pupils think. Hence chapter 1, but we shall return to that.

However else one may be tackling the issue in one's own classroom or curriculum area, a school policy about 'race' is a useful thing. To state this is not to claim that all policies are effective, or that their establishment is any kind of end in itself, but it is to claim that given the structure of most schools' decision-making and the struggle for legitimacy that antiracist work has to go through, getting an institutional policy is a useful process and a worthwhile target.

Paraphrasing some comments of Robin Richardson's about LEA policies, we might say the following about a school policy:

— it is a resource for advocates, in that it provides legitimacy for their concerns, that is, it gives them protection from certain criticisms and scepticisms, and it gives them a fuller and more rational hearing in debates and deliberations;

— it is an internal communication between different levels of power in the school, and may contribute to procedural, structural and cultural change within the school (Richardson, 1983; 1990).

In addition, many people have found that the process of debating and deciding upon some sort of policy has been valuable in itself. It seems to clarify issues and make people think out where they stand.

Such advantages may appeal to 'advocates', but there are also arguments which can be put to those who are initially uninterested. One might be that in a contentious and newly recognised area of concern, staff need both guidance and the process of debate to clarify their aims and practices. Another is that a school's principles need formalising and setting down — they have to be nowadays in prospectuses and school development plans in any case — so that pupils, parents, and new staff know what the school stands for.

As arguments of principle these are uncontentious enough, but efforts to get a policy statement on something the staff as a whole consider irrelevant will fall on stony ground. Although, as Richardson suggests, a policy confers some legitimacy on the debate, some degree of legitimacy has to be established in the first place for there even to be a policy. 'Race' may be a recognised area of concern nationally but for many teachers it is not so in their own school. Thus the problem is how to get 'race' on the agenda in a white school, how to get past the inertia produced by the statement 'but there's no problem here'.

Policies in multiracial schools

Perhaps there are some lessons to be learnt from multiracial schools. It may be thought that there is a difference between successful strategies for getting a policy in schools where there are Asian and black pupils and those where there are few or none, yet surprisingly this does not appear to be so. The expectation that it might arises from the assumption that those working in multiracial schools would see some issues more clearly, and, in particular, would recognise the curriculum opportunities of a multicultural society more easily. As already argued in chapter 3 however, there is a sense in which although the presence of black or Asian children has made 'race' an issue, the issue has been mostly conceived as being to do with them and not with us. Many substantially black schools now recognise the implicit racism of this formulation of 'the problem', but as long as white schools see the issue that way they will understandably see no implications for themselves.

By no means a majority of largely or substantially black/Asian schools have explicit policies about 'race', but among those which have, there are some patterns to be seen in how the policies are phrased and argued. In looking at the first that appeared — mostly in the early to mid 1980s — we can see what the formulators and the staffs which accepted them saw as the key issues.

A simple content analysis of these policies reveals some interesting emphases. All began by stressing the existence and undesirability of racist attitudes and behaviour in either the pupils or the immediate locality. One began:

> Due to the increased electoral success of the National Front, ... staff ...(should)... make a special effort to combat the evils of racism.

It then details an NF leaflet which was found in the school, arguing that its discovery makes it necessary to have a school policy.

84

Racialism outside schools is becoming gradually more respectable and this development will inevitably have repercussions inside schools.

The rest of the document scarcely mentions the curriculum. It is couched in terms of reacting in a disciplinary and guidance sense to a threat, a threat to the black pupils in the school and to the assumed values of the school by the rejection of these values by many white pupils. Another began with an account of an Asian pupil having his throat cut by skinheads. The remainder of the document was almost entirely about the containment and reaction to expressions of racism by pupils.

A third very well known school detailed the forms of racism encountered by its pupils. It briefly mentioned that it acknowledged and valued all pupils' cultures, and its first point was about getting people's names right. The discussion then turned to physical attacks, intimidation, verbal abuse, racist literature, and racially exclusive behaviour. What was suggested for incorporation into the school's code of practice is a set of guidelines for dealing with racist incidents.

Another school whose policy said a good deal more about the curriculum and its role in combating racism, nonetheless set the agenda initially as being a response to the 'racist incidents and expressions of racism that have occurred in and around the school', such as verbal abuse, physical attacks, distribution of racist publications, wearing NF and BNP insignia, and graffiti.

A fifth school argued the same way. Its policy statement began with the question 'Why the need for a policy statement?' and answered it by pointing to the frequency of racist incidents like name-calling, graffiti, racist jokes, and the threatening and perpetration of violence.

Despite the lack of any substantial discussion of the curriculum in the early policy statements, the point is that these schools, that is the activists in the schools who actually drafted the policy statements, either conceived the main imperative as dealing with the expressions of overt racism in the pupils, or decided that defining the imperative that way would be more persuasive and compelling to others.

The imperative does not seem to have been conceived in terms of golden new enriching curriculum opportunities, the possibilities of broadening the cultural base of the classroom to make education more fulfilling for everyone. This kind of rationale is often advanced, but in many schools well known for their work on 'race', it does not seem to have been a strong enough force to get anything changed.

Let me be clear that this is not intended as any kind of criticism of those who worked to bring about these policy statements. When faced daily with the victims of overt racism there should be no doubt where the first imperative for action is. Having raised the issue this way, the schools all went on to reappraise their priorities in the curriculum. This shows something of the differences between the older 'celebrating diversity' and integrationist approaches and an antiracist approach. The extent of racism among whites ought to be an incentive for us to do something about it, to do otherwise is really not to grasp the educational nettle.

That being the case, we have to try to clarify the most effective strategy for those in white areas concerned to raise the issue of 'race'. We must be clear what the issue is. Is it that a richer, broader curriculum awaits us if we only had less ethnocentrist eyes to see it? This is positive, optimistic reasoning, presenting a multicultural approach as an opportunity, not a threat. There are times when it must be sold this way, and if presented like this it may reduce the anxiety and resultant hostility in many teachers. We should not be under any illusions, however, that the world is really such a happy place. If schools which were largely Asian or black failed to respond in this way for twenty years or more, if they found that even with black children in their classrooms they began to get policies only when these pupils were the victims of racist violence, it may be naive to think that a more positive approach will work elsewhere. If it took people having their throats cut by young fascists to enable antiracist teachers to get multiracial schools' policies through, one has to be something of an optimist to expect a more far-sighted approach in white schools.

Policy formation in a white school

Having thus argued for posing the issues in a certain way, it may be instructive to look at the process of trying to get an antiracist policy in some largely white schools. Reflection on case studies coupled with the experiences of the schools mentioned above may produce some general guidelines for action.

The first school concerned was a large comprehensive in a town with a population of about 120,000, with a small proportion of black or Asian people and a smaller proportion still in the school. A very small number of staff out of a total of about seventy were concerned about racism to the extent of seeing it as an educational issue which affected them: its most common expression would be found in the kind of attitudes expressed in the pupils' writings referred to in chapter 1. The kind of racist political activity noted by several of the London schools mentioned earlier, was also in evidence in the area outside the school. A small core of boys were members of the National Front or had some allegiance to the now defunct British Movement, and not only were they evangelising among the other pupils, they were doing so in an informational vacuum left by the school. The evangelising was not on a large scale and was fairly secretive, but this capitalised on the slight glamour these organisations already had as tough and violent, giving affiliates a feeling of being one of the elect.

Although several staff would have described themselves as antiracists, and were indeed involved in antiracist work outside, it took this growing racist activity to focus the issue for them inside the school. They would have welcomed an earlier catalyst, and today might not need one, but at the time they saw this as a personal and institutional spur to action. This particular spur to action would have been hard to present as a positive opportunity for enriching the curriculum; it was unpleasant and perni-cious, and the only way to get any kind of staff support for action seemed to be to show them the kind of racism that was coming to the surface in the school.

There were regular staff meetings where almost anything could be discussed (after the most vital issues of corridor supervision and the best system of queuing for lunch), but action was more likely to follow from staff meeting discussion if the matter had first been discussed by, and perhaps been the subject of recommendations from, the meetings of two of the centres of power in the school: the year heads and the Heads of Department. Accordingly, a file of National Front and British Movement literature was put together, not all of it taken from pupils in the school but all of it certainly available to them, and a special meeting was asked for with the year heads, who met weekly during a lunch hour.

The extent to which such initiatives seem to depend on individuals is disturbing, but it was clear that not just anyone could go to the year heads' meeting and expect to be listened to with much patience. Teaching is often tough and wearing, and committed, concerned and hard working as these year heads were, it was understandable that they should want to minimise any new problem if at all possible. Thus, whoever presented this 'new' problem to them had to be credible in terms of hard work, competence, experience and realism. Fortunately there was a head of department (also thought of as a future year head) who was able to able to attend the meeting and speak about the issue. Although the convenor of the year heads' group, the pastoral deputy head, was politely accommodating while actually being cynical, there were two clear allies amongst the group of eight who were pressed in advance to attend and be supportive in the meeting, which in the end lasted no more than 25 minutes. It was nevertheless valuable to have the examples of racist leaflets, since none of the year heads had actually seen any of the material before. (It is remarkable how many people of liberal persuasion give lip service to opposing far right parties, but support their 'freedom of speech' in the belief that they engage in the same kind of political discourse as the other political parties. They are usually shocked to read the kind of thing printed in the fringe right-wing press, which does not mince words.)

This was the first step, and, clearly, all that was being done at this stage was to sensitise people to the crudest, most blatant forms of racism and try to get them to take action against them. Perhaps the more subtle manifestations need a tuned ear. The year heads felt that the racism of the kind in the literature was the most visible and pointed tip of an iceberg, but that there was a limit to what they could do about it. They could confiscate racist material, they could suspend distributors (or those carrying the little stickers which had begun to appear around the school), but they preferred to rely if possible on the existing school ban against any political activity rather than to act explicitly against racism. The head was reported to be willing to back temporary suspension for offenders.

The year heads were right to say there was a limit to what they could do about it, and there is also a limit to how much policies, as outlined earlier, can do about racist pupils. In so far as the school has a role in creating and reinforcing racist beliefs reflected elsewhere in pupils' families, the media, and in peer groups, all those with pastoral responsibilities can do is mop up after the mess left by the holes in the curriculum. The year heads in this school accepted that they had a role to play, but they were quick to say that the manifestations of racism which they, as links in the disciplinary chain had to deal with, had their origins and proper solutions elsewhere.

The issue of racist attitudes was then raised at a staff meeting, after a half-hearted attempt by the head to 'forget' about it by pretending it was the subject of a local heads' meeting. It was not, but what was going on was the well-known management ploy of sitting on or ignoring controversy if at all possible. Heads cannot do much right in the eyes of the 'public', and if a school is at all worried about its reputation (and this one was) it does not do to be making a stand about anything 'controversial'.

Plans had been too well laid, however. Half a dozen staff had been asked to state their concern about racism among the pupils if the opportunity arose in the staff meeting. They were all people who recognised that there was a problem, but were not necessarily those who always came to or spoke at staff meetings. They were asked to couch their comments in terms of asking for guidance from the head, rather than attacking him with demands that he should do something. They were also asked not to sit together so they would not appear as an identifiable group.

It is interesting to note the way in which many school staff meetings work. Most have no formal system of voting and reflect the essentially autocratic nature of school management. Balances of opinion are hard to quantify and their quantification by voting is frequently resisted by heads, because they can then listen to whom they choose and still claim to be 'sensing the feeling of the meeting'. (This is not meant to sound as if all heads are by nature dictators it is often a role which is forced upon them.) At any rate, such a way of conducting a meeting is open to manipulation by several staff agreeing to all speak in the same way and a small number of people can thereby create 'the feeling of the meeting'. There is no doubt that such a technique is undemocratic, even Machiavellian, but so is the usual alternative.

At the meeting some staff felt this was really nothing more than a general issue of politeness, and that pupils who did not open doors for staff were the same ones who called others names. Others saw the racial abuse as no worse than fat children being called names. All the same, the stage had been set, and more people than expected joined in, so it would have been hard for the head to have made no response. The response was to ask the head of departments' meeting to discuss the matter — the matter being fairly loosely defined as overt racism among the pupils.

The HoD who had attended the year heads' meeting again presented the problem in a deliberately immediate and accessible way, highlighting the effect of pupils' racism on the small number of black and Asian pupils, and on the white pupils themselves. The fact that some pupils strongly believe something so antithetical to liberal values can be a useful lever on otherwise conventional staff. Their liberalism can be mobilised, since if they can be convinced of the strength and the nature of pupil attitudes they cannot but seek to respond in some way. By this time, unfortunately, the folder of racist literature was no longer available, since the head said he had lost it.

Each department head was asked to take back to their department meetings four brief examples of racist comments or incidents and to come back with a departmental response to each one. This was intended to provide a focus so that people were talking about the same thing, and to tease out more of what people really thought.

Although two departments reported that they had never come across such incidents and that there was therefore not much of a problem (all the examples had in fact happened in the previous few months) no one recommended inaction and a draft policy statement was circulated (full details in Gaine, 1987, though useful model school statements can be found in the NUT's booklet *Antiracism in Education* (1989) and in a similar and very detailed booklet produced by what was AMMA — now the ATL.

The school was really not an especially radical one, but the strategy worked. There was discussion, naturally, about the proposed policy statement, but discussions were becoming fruitful. These processes are by no means valuable only for their end products. The exchanges, alliances and insights which arise during the consultation and discussion stages are of lasting value. Typically in a busy school the discussion was guillotined by the caretaker since it had been the last item on a long agenda, but a small group was asked to spend some more time on the wording, which was later refined to a point where it achieved general consent.

Ironically, having gone so far along the road of being one of the first white schools to have such a policy, it went no further because of various actions by the head. This shows, of course how crucial their role is in any such development. He had been nervous all along about the school producing anything in writing, in case the papers or the governors made something 'controversial' out of it. The increasing necessity for schools to 'market' themselves makes the head's nervousness quite realistic. It was also feared that an unfavourable portrayal of the school as an antiracist one would have given pupils' job chances with many local employers the kiss of death. The head actually said, though not in public, that however good the 'cause' he would not let the school take any publicly contentious stance lest its reputation suffered. This is the sharp end of any debate about schools being answerable to society: however ostrich-like or bigoted the often self-appointed spokespeople of 'society' may be, schools do not have the power to ignore them.

A broadly similar account is given by Roberts (1988) and Massey (1991) about their own two schools in Hampshire. In Massey's, the level and nature of racist attitudes amongst pupils was utterly typical of what could be found in white schools the length and breadth of the country:

> These pupils would profess a belief in the importance of tolerance and admit that prejudice was wrong. Racist views were presented with a certain respectability and the necessity of the expulsion of non-whites was expressed with regret. However, such actions were seen as inevitable due to the immigrants' unwillingness to give up their customs and religion and to prevent further unemployment (1991, p.128).

Though several key staff were supportive of some kind of policy development, it took months of meetings, visits to other schools and research by a working party to settle on the most effective strategy. Training for a small number was rejected on the basis of its limited likely effect. Focusing on extreme Right literature was rejected because it did not reflect the views of many pupils in the school. Inviting in an outsider to lead some kind of awareness-raising or training event as a catalyst was also rejected, on grounds that no outsider would have sufficient credibility to persuade and carry along enough staff without antagonising them. In the end they got the head's agreement for a half-day closure and the consequent two-hours of inset time. This was scrupulously carefully planned, dividing the staff into cross-curricular groups, with a member of the working party taking each group through brainstorming on key ideas, informed by accounts of pupils' views, with opportunities for staff to voice anxieties and experiences.

Their working party is a good example of how the processes of discussion, collaboration and the gradual involvement of more people can produce progress of itself. The activity in the school had come to the attention of the LEA, who were impressed and interested, and this gave the 'activists' more credibility.

The head finished the inset day with a statement that racism was now firmly on the school's agenda, and after more meetings the working party settled on a dual strategy of producing a policy and winning more in-service time for curriculum development in the area. It took time, over two years, but the in-service happened and was positively evaluated. The policy the working party wanted was approved by the governors, and accepted by the staff.

A grim example of what can go wrong is the account from Burnage School in Manchester (Macdonald et al, 1989), referred to in chapter three. *Murder in the Playground* was commissioned as an investigation into the murder of one pupil by another in a largely working class boys' school with a significant proportion of Asian pupils. It is a detailed account of how the head and a deputy had instituted a kind of antiracist 'policy' which clearly did no good and generated destructive opposition from some staff, as well as rather crudely alienating some white boys in the school. The details are much too long to summarise, but the relevant section is well worth reading in conjunction with the points made about strategy in the next chapter.

Chapter 6

Changing Your School: Futures

This chapter sums up what seem to me some of the key factors in getting things moving — or frustrating developments — in largely white schools, in short: a list of catalysts and obstacles. It is to some extent impressionistic rather than the outcome of systematic enquiry but it is based on association with and discussions in dozens of schools in the past few years, as well as familiarity with the relevant literature. Further thoughts and strategies about policy development can be found in Gaine, and Lyseightjones, both in Cole (1989); George (1993); Macdonald et al (1989); NUT (1993); Richardson (1985); Runnymede Trust (1993). The points made here are summarised in two flow charts later.

Let us assume the initial catalyst is an individual or small group who want to bring about some change, in which case there are three prerequisites. Firstly, they need a plan, certainly for the term ahead and loosely at least thereafter. A plan is necessary from the organisational point of view but also for morale: change can be slow and frustrating, but less so if we have a long-term strategy. Reading other people's accounts (like those in the previous chapter) can be very useful in formulating a plan and timetable of action, comparing and considering which features are different and which might work the same way in one's own school, and noticing the sorts of things which go wrong.

The second prerequisite is support. This may come from inside the school but, if not, is worth seeking from others in similar schools, people contacted through correspondence, contacts through the local Racial Equality Council or a teachers' union, a librarian, someone in the LEA advisory/inspection service (if they still have one), a kindred spirit in a local college or university education department, or just friends!

The other prerequisite is in a way a combination of the above two: a working group. There are, of course, situations where someone is working alone, at least in their own school, but even then it is important to discuss strategy with other people. The working group might become a formal working party or exist as an informal strategy and support group.

Key factors on the way to initial change

These three prerequisites aside, this next list is of factors which can be helpful or not, depending on how they apply. All are worth considering in any initial planning.

National climate about education and 'race' — politically, and in terms of media agendas and current furores. Obviously this is built into the National Curriculum and is fixed to an extent, and the national climate is far worse than many would like. Yet there are moments when opportunities can be seized: concern about the election of a neo-fascist London councillor, or high profile racist activity in Germany, or the free schools viewing which Speilberg arranged for his film 'Schlinder's List', might all provide a more willing audience for a while.

National Policy — this is distinguished from 'climate' because of the gap which often exists between formal statements by the likes of SCAA and the more media-conscious pronouncements by ministers. The former is strictly policy and likely to be pursued explicitly, the latter is 'climate': a mood, a setting of key rhetorical agendas. In practice, both are policy with different degrees of overtness and formality and at times the latter is more important in determining events (witness the events in Brent described in chapter three). Nevertheless, formal national policy has to be used for all it is worth to claim legitimacy, and the best quick summary of this will be found in Runnymede Trust (1993) pp.5-9.

LEA policy —this gives formal legitimacy nearer at hand, but is less of a factor than it used to be. Some LEAs, like Hampshire, Northamptonshire and Hertfordshire have sound policies in place which lay certain clear obligations on schools, though no new policies are likely to emerge from the disempowered and unfunded LEAs of the 1990s.

Local climate about 'race' — this may involve local folklore about 'good' schools, the varying presence of Asian and black pupils, or any issues which have arisen (perhaps publicly) in neighbouring schools — perhaps about RE and the law.

Relative autonomy/immunity from inhibiting pressures... like the local media, hostile governors or parents. This may depend on the above and whether some local incident has sensitised potential opposition, as well as factors like the credibility of the people involved and their formal and informal support.

The involvement of someone relatively senior and respected among the staff, so the initiative cannot be written off as the naive concern of a few inexperienced 'youngsters.' Heads are crucial in any school development, but they need not be involved at an early stage. If they are indifferent or oppositional then it is even more important to have someone with credibility 'on board'.

The involvement of the key power and opinion blocs like year and curriculum leaders. You might be lucky and have commitment from some of these initially, but at some early stage of the overall strategy they need to be persuaded.

Potential allies in informal power blocs amongst staff: the micropolitics of the school. In practice, some things do not get done or changed much without such support. Whatever someone's formal status, if their competence or wisdom as a teacher is respected their support is invaluable. Lyseight-jones (1989, p.41) suggests classifying the staff into supporters, blockers, opinion leaders and don't-knows before you start, then further identifying the bandwagoners and laggards amongst the supporters.

The formal and informal status of 'activists' can get one a hearing, or not. Classically, the newly qualified teacher who is actively involved in the union, flaunts the informal dress code amongst the staff, challenges sexist language and has an anti-nuclear sticker on her/his Citroen 2CV gets listened to less and less (unless they shout). The rest of the staff are likely to see the initiative not as a 'just cause' but as 'just another cause'. This might very easily be read as a reactionary injunction not to rock the boat too much, but it's entirely about tactics, not principles.

A 'hero' (or shero) teacher: someone to whom the issue is so important that they work tirelessly at it, bringing about change partly through moral force but also by doing others' work for them. Such a person needs or earns the credibility already referred to and can be immensely effective, though structures and procedures need to established so that everything does not wither when they leave...

The presence of racist activity in the school — it seems paradoxical to regard this as a 'helpful' factor, but it is the most obvious evidence against the 'no problem here' syndrome.

The opportunity for all staff to discuss the matter in sub-groups, especially in large schools, thus increasing the chances of any final decision feeling 'owned.' This may be self-evident but it is very important to structure developments so that plenty of focused discussion is possible: a small group pushing a policy through does not tend to produce any worthwhile lasting results.

The provision of more than one focus for discussion, such as racist literature amongst pupils (new to most staff), case studies, pupils' views, or curriculum ideas. This is examined a little more in the section on in-service.

In areas where there are **black and Asian** people in any numbers, can you meet with their **organisations**, hear what they have to say, enlist their support?

The new presence of a small number of black or Asian pupils — when this happens, perhaps because of reorganisation as well as population changes, things might go on just as before. Or it can raise awareness or problems and conflicts within staff and pupils.

The new arrival of head or senior staff from a more aware school or multiracial area. It is hard to quantify the effect of this across the country, but it is certainly a good conduit of ideas and insights and is likely to make

96

for a more sympathetic senior audience for a concerned group of staff (if the new head is not the change agent her/himself, which sometimes happens). It can also mean there is a powerful ally in governors' meetings.

Innovative Head/senior staff — though 'top down' initiatives without proper grounding do not tend to be popular or effective, heads with real commitment to this issue and who carry their staffs with them probably bring about the most effective school change.

The normal structure/operation of the school facilitates innovation and allows issues to surface. In a rigidly and hierarchically managed school, with firm control from the top about the issues which are allowed to surface and which are suppressed, you will have to put up a fight.

The issue is raised in a way which avoids initial hostility — it is very hard for white people not to feel accused when British racism is being discussed, and doubly hard if the people are teachers being implicitly told about something they could do better. The section on in-service has some suggestions here.

A respected, not too threatening, non-secretive working group which ensures that whatever it lays on for staff is done well. Several of the previous points key in with this one.

Absence of other powerfully prioritised issues, like revising the National Curriculum — again. In its worst form the opposite of this is the Doctrine of the Unripe Time: 'Yes I agree with you we ought to make some changes, but not now, not yet.' So many issues are prioritised for schools and teachers that it would be unrealistic to pretend we set our own agendas, but it would be equally unrealistic to try to claim time and space for an antiracist development when other major changes are going on. There are those who argue that the best time to make changes is when everything is destabilised and many other changes are happening, but I find it hard to agree.

Some critical incident or event, like a serious case of harassment (which usually takes most people by surprise) or a personal experience affecting the life of the school, can raise questions, awareness, and change priorities.

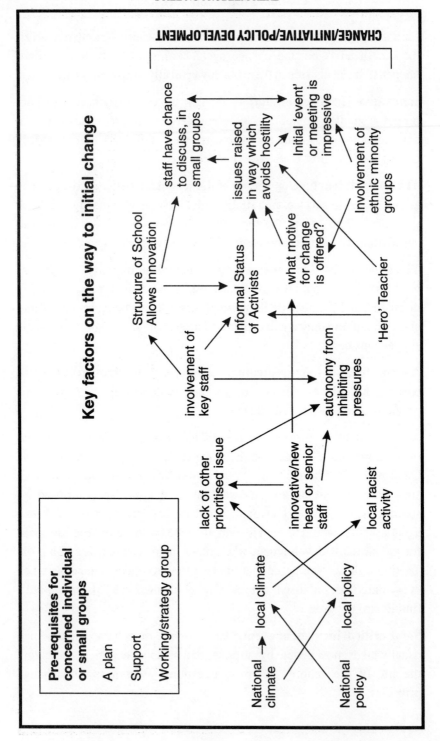

Key factors on the way to initial change

CHANGE/INITIATIVE/POLICY DEVELOPMENT

Pre-requisites for
concerned individual
or small groups

A plan

Support

Working/strategy group

staff have chance
to discuss, in
small groups

Initial 'event'
or meeting is
impressive

Involvement of
ethnic minority
groups

Structure of School
Allows Innovation

issues raised
in way which
avoids hostility

what motive
for change
is offered?

Informal Status
of Activists

'Hero' Teacher

involvement of
key staff

autonomy from
inhibiting
pressures

lack of other
prioritised issue

innovative/new
head or senior
staff

local racist
activity

National → local climate
climate

local policy

National
policy

98

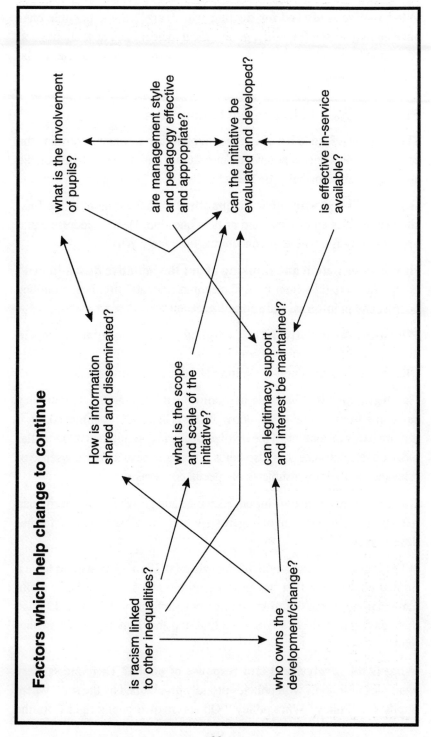

Factors which help change to continue

what is the involvement of pupils?

are management style and pedagogy effective and appropriate?

can the initiative be evaluated and developed?

is effective in-service available?

How is information shared and disseminated?

what is the scope and scale of the initiative?

can legitimacy support and interest be maintained?

is racism linked to other inequalities?

who owns the development/change?

What motive is offered for dealing with 'race'? Some possible ones have already arisen (morality, policy, local incident and how about good education?) and chapter one describes my own, but motives cannot be taken for granted.

Factors which help change to continue

There is then a second list of questions about factors which determine the course of events once a policy or a curriculum initiative is actively on the agenda, or more formally, on the school's development plan.

Is racism linked with other inequalities? Discussed more in the final chapter but it is an obvious and critical question. Do you address equal opportunities as a whole or concentrate on 'race'? Why?

How is information and thinking about the initiative disseminated? Is the issue a regular item in staff meetings, parents' circulars, on notice boards, and in informal staffroom discussions?

Who owns the initiative? This is the outcome of some of the factors in the first list: if it's owned by someone who lacks credibility, or someone who then leaves, or a non-consulting Head, then it will not stick.

Can legitimacy for the issue be maintained? Again, initial legitimacy can come from several of the above factors (like NCC documents) but it is more likely to continue if the involvement and commitment of particular individuals legitimate it. It also helps if teachers have a growing sense of relevance to their own subjects or special concerns.

Can the initiative be developed, ie change and grow? A longer term plan may be needed here, involving review and the expectation of further development.

What is the scale and scope of the initiative? It may be wise to have a limited objective at first, for instance within one subject area, or about name-calling, or multifaith assemblies, or reading materials, with the hope that others will come to see this as a first step and the necessity for further ones.

What is the involvement and response of pupils? There are salutary examples of schools with policies proudly proclaimed by the staff, where pupils say 'Policy? What policy?' Others involve pupils right from the first, and indeed some would argue that this is a prerequisite of a genuine egalitarian initiative (see, for example Epstein, 1993).

Is there any means of judging the initiative's effect — in attitudes, behaviour, or both? This cannot usually be answered in the early stages and is not accessible by crude indices in any case, but written examples of pupils' (and staff's?) comments with a two or three year gap would provide some measure. This is seldom done.

Is the curriculum content and the pedagogy appropriate for what we want to achieve? It is worth while asking this of my own 'classroom' chapters in *No Problem Here* and there are useful self-critical curriculum/pedagogy accounts in Naidoo (1992), Epstein (1993), Massey (1989), and Cohen (in Donald and Rattansi, 1992).

One of the key areas in the diagram is **in-service and staff development**, since there is no doubt that teachers' in-service courses about 'race' can have positive effects. If well-planned, focused on needs and well taught or led, they have the potential to change teachers' and schools' practices for the better. They are not easy to plan or run. They are not the same as courses on primary science or teaching Shakespeare, because like Standard English and assessment, 'race' touches many of our deepest preconceptions. One implication of this is that learning is likely to be a mixture of flashes or spurts and many slower increments, and is likely to carry an emotional charge.

Though individuals still go on courses to follow their own interests, in-service is increasingly school-based and related to the school's development plan. There are trainers, lecturers and LEA staff who run suitable training days, though we are often expensive and can use a small school's annual in-service budget in one bite, so the activist or working party is increasingly in the daunting position of planning and leading a day or half-day training event for their own colleagues.

A useful precursor and frequent catalyst for such an event is a course which an individual volunteer teacher has attended or studied, like the the Open University's *'Race', Education and Society* or individual modules on many MEds. There are fewer such courses of any length than there were, and while they help give the necessary confidence they are becoming more of a luxury.

The potential difficulties of setting up in-service development for one's colleagues are obvious: confidence, credibility, and the need for continued coexistence after the event, might sum them up. Nevertheless, it can be done very effectively, and there are several purchasable handbooks which give detailed guidance for relative beginners. These handbooks are best examined for oneself and decisions and choices made according to individual circumstances. Most suggest possible plans and structures for day or half-day courses, with hand-outs and timing, and all are produced by people with considerable experience of leading them. I offer a few comments about each at the end of this chapter.

In the meantime, I have some general observations about planning a half-day or day course for a school or a cluster of schools (developed from my own introduction to the Longman Pack). They are set out on pages 103-109 and followed with an annotated list of resources to support a course of this kind.

What are you going to cover?

The most obvious question here is whether to address 'race' separately or to have a general equal opportunities approach. This is not necessarily an issue of depth versus breadth, since there are those who argue that racism is better understood when examined simultaneously with sexism. I touch on this in the final chapter, and it is well explored in Rosalyn George's handbook. It is worth saying that outcomes are unpredictable: I can recall an occasion where the simultaneous coverage of 'race', class and gender on a primary school's Professional Development Day was really exciting and useful, but in another school there was some (unexplained) deep current about 'race' which suddenly ignited and really needed a day's focused work even to get started.

There is a further question about whether to deal with the formal and the hidden curriculum simultaneously, for example, book selection and racial harassment. Clearly they are connected, but it may be strategic to focus on harassment and let the participants point out the links to the taught curriculum (or vice versa), thus themselves defining the need for a further session.

Another strategy is to include equal opportunities or racism as as aspect of some other theme: a secondary-primary group of schools in Crawley recently had a joint in-service day on self-esteem, with optional work-shops on gender and self-esteem, 'race' and self-esteem, and so on.

Who will be there?

Almost all the training days I have done have been for teachers only. Though there are obvious reasons for including governors and all staff who have contact with pupils, it is also true to say that not everyone's training needs are the same: teachers may want to examine classroom processes at their level of expertise without explaining everything to the cook or to the bank manager who chairs the governors' finance committee. The dynamics of formal status (and probably gender) are very likely to marginalise some non-teaching staff or keep them quiet in discussions. I have seen training days where the secretaries felt alienated by the 'waffle' the teachers felt comfortable with, and where the teachers felt intimidated by the silent listening of the chair of governors. On the other hand, I recently facilitated an equal opportunities training day for an Anglican primary school (though in fact it was entirely planned by the deputy head). The day opened with written comments collected from Asian parents and the results of a questionnaire given to children about their perceptions of gender differences in the school, so we began by hearing from the only two groups not present. Everyone else was: some governors, the chair of the Parent Teacher Association, two local priests, the dinner staff, caretaker, secretary, non-teaching assistants, special needs assistants and all the teachers. The activities had to take the very mixed group into account, so they focused on overall assumptions about gender, 'race' and ability, ways of responding to particular sorts of incidents, very general points about the selection of books and materials. Most of the work was in small groups. It was a model of good practice and did a great deal for relationships in the school, but it took hours of planning, careful consideration of activities and group composition, and of course money to pay the non-teaching staff overtime.

Most schools in this country have a white staff, and where there are black and Asian teachers they are almost always in a minority. If there is an Asian or black member of staff, their role in an in-service programme needs careful thought. Such teachers are in a difficult position:

— if vocal they run the risk of being seen as 'having a chip on their shoulder';

— if silent they may be blamed for not being helpful about something about which they are 'expert';

— if they talk about painful experiences they are probably making themselves more vulnerable than the white people present;

— if asked to speak or comment by one of the participants it may be that they are being asked to be spokesperson for everyone black or Asian;

— they may survive in a largely white environment by 'keeping their heads down' and may be ambivalent about what sort of line to take with colleagues when 'race' gets a public airing;

— if they, and not a white member of staff front the day, does that mean racism is a black or Asian person's problem? They will also get any emotional flak and could be blamed for creating a problem where there wasn't one, special pleading etc.

In schools where there are several black and/or Asian members of staff it is impossible to generalise about the dynamics of who says/leads what and how it will be received, though it clearly needs thrashing out by the interested staff before any inset day.

Practicalities

If people are to work in groups it is worth giving careful thought to the group make-up. It might be decided to let participants form their own groups, but it needs a positive decision.

Have a range of short but authoritative articles available to which you can refer people. The Longman pack has a few fact sheets; *Equality Assurance* (Runnymede Trust, 1993) has some excellent single-page checklists and summaries; Runnymede Trust's *Different Worlds* (1986) is digestible, brief and authoritative; their *Multi-Ethnic Britain: Facts and Trends* (1994) even more so, and the journal *Multicultural Teaching* has a rich vein of thirteen years' editions with many useful and well focused articles.

If one person is carrying most of the anxiety about whether the day is going well, then practicalities like drinks and lunch need to run smoothly.

Statement of aims

These are the aims of the organisers not the whole staff's, since they may not all have wanted such a session in the first place. Make them simple but state them clearly at the beginning, maybe visually on an OHP/flip chart/poster.

Suggestions:

— to raise awareness about multicultural education/racism to help in staffroom discussion;

— to prepare the ground for making our curriculum more multicultural (or effective in countering racism?) where possible;

— to air some issues so we can all see where we stand, as a staff;

— to try to clarify some concerns which have been troubling some members of staff;

— to see if we are meeting the requirements of the National Curriculum;

— to examine the relevance of multicultural perspectives (racism?) in an all-white school.

Preparing yourself

Let us assume that the person leading the session...

...is interested but not a specialist
...is a member of staff of the school involved and not used to leading the staff in an in-service capacity
...no formal time for follow-up has been agreed.

Bear in mind that the vast majority of teachers find this topic at least mildly threatening and can easily be made to feel accused (and hence either defensive or aggressive.) They might in some schools be in teaching situations they are unsure of — having in practice to make policy decisions about home languages or religious observances which may be ducked or fudged by government, LEAs or heads.

Also, many do not feel on safe ground so may say little. The more ignorant/de-skilled we feel, the harder it is for us to be open to learning anything.

We are also all prey to the many myths and stereotypes about 'race' that abound in Britain.

Strategy

All this means that the talking that is done in a large group can be a mixture of:

apparently unprompted anecdotes or assurances that 'I'm not at all racist';
resentful accounts of conflicts or dilemmas people have had;
cautious, nervous, playing safe;
recitation of commonly held myths or assumptions...

Ideally, creating a sense of common purpose, and hence trust, is a way through these potential blockages and diversions, but it would be naive to suggest that this can be reliably generated in a fairly short workshop.

Let them talk...

Choose activities which give space for people to talk (in a structured and focused way) in small groups. They need to do this, and it is far more effective to have targeted talk than to take up particular issues in a larger group.

Nevertheless, while 'touring' small groups at work, or in plenary or feedback sessions, some predictable issues will probably come up. The issues are always complex, are seldom resolvable by a single factual answer, and usually spring from one of the emotional factors mentioned above (resentment, uncertainty, confusion).

Watch out for diversions.

If people feel uncomfortable, or want to avoid examining something which challenges them, they might intellectualise

'....Well of course Fanon looked into this years ago, and I think his explanation is very useful....'

or go on a world tour

'....Are we really any worse than other countries, I mean racism is pretty rife in France isn't it?'

'....Don't you think we need to understand what's going on in Bosnia (Los Angeles/Lebanon/Berlin/Delhi/Turkey etc...)'

or point the finger

'....But what about conflict between Muslims and Hindus? That's the real problem, and I know a Pakistani whose father won't let her even talk to West Indians....'

or dig (and re-dig) a defensive ditch around themselves

'....As I said before, I don't really understand this, I'm sure I wasn't brought up with any racist ideas, and I've worked abroad where I found we all mixed together quite happily....'

Some responses:

To intellectualisers and tourists...

'Yes it's a big issue, but I think we sometimes hide from it by over-theorising or looking for motes in others' eyes. After all, our responsibility is the education of pupils in this country and in this school....'

To finger-pointers...

'We aren't responsible for what Sikhs feel about Muslims, (or whatever) and maybe it's not in our power to do anything directly about it. What aspects of racism do we have any power to influence or change?'

To self-defence specialists...

Stating and owning your own prejudices can be quite disarming. If someone tells me they are not a racist I try to tell them some of the racist ideas I (and doubtless they) learned as they grew up. Some films make this point well, see 'No Problem Here' below. As for 'I can't be racist because I've got black friends' the best reply I have heard is 'That's like saying I can't be a sexist because my mother was a woman'.

To difficult questioners...

a) Ask a question in return...
highlighting something in the question which has not been thought through, for example, someone asks:

'Don't you think there's a bit too much of a tendency for people to stick to ways they've brought over here, rather than be like us... etc...'

a reply might be:

'...How does that apply to a British-born Muslim? Which ways should they 'stick' to?' or

'I have a bit of a problem with 'us'. Does it not include Jews, atheists, Catholics of Polish and Irish descent, communists? Lesbians?'

b) Challenge or deflect?
You need to be familiar with factual information about some of the more common myths, but obviously you cannot expect to put paid to all of them. It is better to refer people to an article or information sheet you have

available rather than enter into a kind of tennis match, trying to counter point for point.

If a myth or stereotype surfaces in a whole-group session ('They're much too involved with crime...') it is probably best to respond with something like 'It confuses things a great deal to make such a sweeping generalisation, it has to be much more complicated than that' or 'I have an information sheet which touches on that to some extent.' This tends to be more effective than arguing a specific point, because where prejudice is concerned your arguer will shift ground if you look like 'winning'.

Having said that, if you are sure of your ground, there are times when it is useful to pursue and highlight a racist argument. You are unlikely to influence the speaker, and may well antagonise her or him (however polite you are) but it can be useful to others to hear the argument and to rehearse for themselves its rebuttal.

If your purpose is training, it is not always useful for you as leader to give vent to your own feelings about a racist remark, but it sometimes is. This dynamic is different depending on whether you are black/Asian or white and you can only play this decision by ear.

c) Refer to group: 'Does anyone else want to comment on that?' 'What does anyone else think?' This may be ineffective, the group may all agree with the comment or not be confident enough to counter it, but it can produce useful dialogue or productive heated argument between people who need to work with each other.

d) Postpone it/file it/re-focus group:

> 'That's an interesting point, and I don't agree, but it's not what our main focus is in the short time we've got today'.

> 'That kind of issue may come in the smaller group discussions later'.

> 'But our main concern today is with our professional concerns in this school in this country....'

Finally, it is worth saying that good workshop materials and activities run themselves, and useful interaction and discussion will have positive benefits which may not be obvious on the day.

Training Packs and Handbooks

Rosalyn GEORGE (1993) A Handbook on Equal Opportunities in Schools, Longman

Perhaps the most comprehensive, this is really a trainer's manual to accompany a separate ring binder of complete training packages on different aspects of equal opportunities. Having said that, it also contains many activities, and rationales/key questions about policies. A particular concern of the author is that inequalities are looked at together rather than separately. Expensive but copyright free.

Chris GAINE, (and Scragg; Burton; Oakes; Basset; Aiken) (1993) Training for Equality, Longman

The ring binder supported by George's book (above). There is a range of starter activities, some longer 'main' activities, and suggested ways of finishing. OHPs, discussion sheets and materials for group work are included. Expensive but copyright free, and you also get similar packages for gender, sexual orientation, mental health and disability.

Jon NIXON, and Mike WATTS, (1989), Whole School Approaches to Multicultural Education, Macmillan

This has good advice to workshop leaders, and different workshops focused on general awareness raising and on curriculum planning, with suggested reading for further ones. It is probably nearer the starting points of those working in urban and multiracial schools.

John TWITCHIN, (1988, 2nd edition 1990) The Black and White Media Book, Trentham.

As the title implies, this is not about school directly but about the media (especially TV), but it contains many suggestions and exercises for workshops and training. It is very good for bringing out all kinds of general assumptions and ideas about 'race'.

Bob McLEAN, and John YOUNG, (1988) Multicultural AntiRacist Education, A Manual for Primary Schools, Longman

This is just what the title claims and has been carefully written to support its reader through a long process of school change. It is very accessibly written, contains many useful and stimulating 'thinking points', has some ready-made exercises to use, and some primary topic web ideas too. Developed in Scotland and obviously had many largely white schools in mind.

Sandi MAITLAND, (1989) Multicultural Inset: a Practical Handbook for Teachers, Trentham

Contains very good, reassuring notes to teachers preparing their school for some inset, particularly putting such teachers as facilitators not experts. On the whole the activities — thoroughly explained and with suggested timings — are about awareness-raising rather than, for instance, curriculum or policy. Out of print but can be found in colleges and teachers' centres.

NEWMAN, E and TRIGGS, P (1991) Equal Opportunities in the Primary School, Bristol Polytechnic

Covers all aspects of equal opportunities, with group activities, checklists and the like. The 'race' parts are brief and rather assume a multiracial school.

NORTHAMPTONSHIRE Inspection and Advisory Service (1991), Racial Harassment

A pack devised by the Inspection and Advisory Service about racial harassment. It includes draft policies, workshop materials and factual information. Well trialled in Northants before publication.

OPEN UNIVERSITY, (1988) Every Child's Language (In-service Pack), OU

This is not exactly a trainer's pack but contains enough material (and tapes) to keep a group occupied for days. For everyone who wants to exploit the possibilities of languages more, even if there is only one bilingual child in the class.

RUNNYMEDE TRUST (1993), Equality Assurance, Runnymede/Trentham

This is a brief but excellent and comprehensive book which tries to bring out all the possibilities for multicultural/antiracist work within the National Curriculum. Runnymede will also supply suggested in-service activities to go with it.

Steve THORP, (1991) Race, Equality and Science Teaching, Association for Science Education

I have seen this snapped up by teachers the moment they see it. It is very thorough and well structured with a good variety of exercises and activities, each with special notes to the facilitator. Many of these are good for general awareness-raising and should be seen as having relevance well beyond any narrow conception of science. It has a companion volume (ASE, 1994) which is more of a practical teachers' manual.

Chris DERRINGTON and Steve THORP (1990) Racism and Travellers, A Training and Discussion pack, Northamptonshire LEA

Though specific, this is ideal for many white areas where the nearest target for racism may be travellers. It contains lots of small group tasks with reflections and advice on how to handle subsequent discussions.

Videos

Apart from Twitchin's book, which by definition uses television a lot, the other training materials tend not to. They have obvious advantages however: they can bring special expertise cheaply and conveniently, they can provide ethnic minority voices and perspectives in largely white areas, and they can present material powerfully. I have listed videos with specialist curriculum expertise under subject headings in the Resources appendix. Videos about racism in mainly white areas are few and far between, but one recent one was made by BBC2. 'No Problem Here?' (30 minutes) was shown in the Western Approach Series (Dorset, Somerset, Devon and Cornwall) in January 1992. Copies may be available from the BBC in Plymouth.

For any introductory course, my own most used video is the film about the American teacher, Jane Elliot, who tells her class of eight year olds that blue-eyed children are superior. The original account was called 'The Eye of the Storm', but there is an updated programme called 'A Class Divided' which includes footage of the original group of children filmed in 1970 interviewed as adults fifteen years later (helpful to those who had doubts about the long term effects). It is old, but never fails to have a powerful effect and can be used to illustrate any inequality: the brown eyed kids could be read as black, or female, or with special needs. It is the most effective film I have come across (out of dozens) for removing that in-service cynicism some staff always seem to have. It doesn't make people feel accused, but it does make them feel. Available from Concord, Felixstowe Road, Ipswich to buy or hire.

The BBC produced many good programmes in the 1980s and 1990s specifically for equal opportunities training. The Mosaic Series focuses on 'race', is generally good and sometimes excellent. There are many specific programmes (on careers for example) and several which could be used as triggers to raise wider issues (like 'Green Pastures, Black

Faces', 'White Politics', in the sub-series of Mosaic called 'Birthrights'.)
I particularly like 'Make it Work', about positive action in employment
taken by some large companies. It does a good demythologising job in
those areas where 'everyone knows' black and Asian people get priority
in jobs. 'Children Without Prejudice' and 'Marked for Life' are about the
early years; 'Painful Lessons' and 'Pakis Go Home' are about harassment.
You can get full details free from Resources for Training, Room G420,
BBC White City, 201 Wood Lane, London W12 7TS.

Chapter 7

Teacher Education

> To say that there is no need to educate all students about such matters because, as one college has said, 'very few of our students go into schools where they are likely to meet mixed classes' is to miss the point... Teachers should be equipped to prepare all their children for life in a multi-racial society. (Select Committee on Race Relations and Immigration, 1969, quoted by Swann Committee, 1985).

One would expect, and indeed hope, that in a society where 'race', ethnicity and culture become issues in schooling they would also be echoed in some way in the education of teachers. In the last fifteen years this has certainly happened, but it has happened simultaneously with other changes, and in some respects 'race' has become symbolic of different models of what teachers ought to be, and hence how they ought to be prepared.

The shape of Initial Teacher Education

The shape and content of Initial Teacher Education (ITE) has gone through many changes during the working lives of teachers practising today. In the immediate post-war years two-year schemes had a necessarily short term emphasis on training and competence, but by the 1960s 'educational studies' had become well established — typically history,

115

philosophy, psychology and sociology. With the three-year certificate rapidly giving way to the first BEds, the education of the 'cultivated man or woman' was emphasised more (and noted with approval by Plowden). Pollard and Tann (1987) suggest that by the late 1960s there 'appeared to be a broad consensus' about good primary practice based on child-centredness, presumably largely facilated by Plowden.

By the late 1970s there was mounting pressure to reform ITE. The real change, with central control and statutory criteria for ITE courses, came about with the establishment of the Committee for the Accreditation of Teacher Education (CATE) in 1984. Though instituted by a Conservative Government, Macintyre (1991), one of its long-serving members, points out that it really had its origins in the 'Great Debate' begun by Callaghan in 1976. In 1977 the DES published a Consultative Document summing up some of the regional conferences resulting from Callaghan's speech. With regard to ITE it noted 'fairly widespread misgivings' on the following issues:

(i) whether entrants to the teaching profession have a sufficient command of the English language and are adequately numerate;

(ii) whether teachers have an adequate appreciation of the world outside the education system, particularly the importance of industry and commerce to the national well-being, and the problems facing an industrial society like ours in an increasingly competitive world;

(iii) whether existing courses of teacher education give enough attention to the role of teachers in a multicultural society;

(iv) whether existing courses of teacher education furnish students with the essential intellectual mastery of the subjects they will teach;

(v) whether they provide students with sufficient practical guidance to enable them to become effective teachers capable of directing children's work and ensuring their good discipline (DES 1977).

Macintyre points to other documents from the late 1970s, mostly from HMI, indicating concerns about ITE, for instance about subject knowledge, teaching methods, assessment, variation between different courses and special educational needs.

Callaghan's concerns were evidently understood in the same terms by the first two Conservative Secretaries of State for Education in the Thatcher administration, and strong continuity was ensured by the role of HMI: they had provided much of the informed evidence that reform was needed; they were significant in shaping the criteria for ITE courses; it was they who visited institutions on CATE's behalf; and it was they who issued 'state of the nation' annual summaries during CATE's lifetime. The Chair of CATE between 1984 and 1993, William Taylor, repeats the argument that this was not a specifically Conservative measure or project:

> The setting up of CATE reflected ... a world-wide concern about the content and quality of teacher preparation. In the United States, in Europe, in Australia, New Zealand, Canada and other economically advanced countries, the seventies saw a series of reports on the needs and shortcomings of teacher preparation which shared many common features (Taylor, 1991, p.111)

The original membership comprised two secondary teachers and two primary; two chief education officers, two LEA elected members, three staff from polytechnics or colleges which undertook ITE, three from universities; one from a large teachers' union; an LEA chief inspector; an educational journalist and two senior industrialists. Indeed Circular 3/84, announcing the establishment of CATE, said

> The membership of the Council will be drawn mainly from practising school teachers, teacher trainers and elected members and officers of local education authorities, with the aim of giving the Secretaries of State the benefit of of the advice of experienced professionals with a broad knowledge of the best practice in teacher education (DES, 1984).

In 1991 Taylor believed that CATE was effective, had produced worthwhile change and had become accepted by the institutions which at first had feared it (it initially withheld accreditation from nine of the first ten institutions it looked at).

Course structures

There remained some diversity in routes to qualified teacher status. Most secondary students did a PGCE. During the 1980s there was a steady increase in the number of primary students training by the PGCE route. Thus by 1990-91 30% of the intake had trained as teachers for only thirty six weeks (Barrett et al, 1992). The majority of primary teachers come from four year BEd courses, typically taught in colleges of higher education or education faculties of the former polytechnics, and a comparative handful — five — in universities giving BA/BSc (QTS) awards.

As regards the subjects student teachers study, it needs to be remembered that to think of BEd as a four year course of ITE is slightly misleading, since by the early CATE criteria two of those years must be spent in academic subject study at the students' own level (though this was subject to some attrition after 1988 due to the demands of the National Curriculum). The structure of these two routes to teaching means that all new teachers will have spent up to half (three-quarters in the case of PGCEs) of their 'training' studying up to three academic subjects at their own level. One change brought about in the 1980s by Keith Joseph was that subject study in any of the social sciences (especially sociology) was not appropriate for teachers, and CATE later restricted subject studies for the primary phase only to those in the National Curriculum.

The model of the teacher

It seems to me that CATE was established at just the time when a non-technicist view of teachers was being formalised and codified — the notion of the reflective practitioner — and that CATE's reformulation in 1989 presaged the ascendancy of a new, more technicist model promoted by the New Right. This has clear implications for teachers' education about 'race' and racism.

The idea of the 'reflective practitioner' was developed initially in the USA by Schon (1983) with reference to the education of professionals, not teachers specifically (though Graves (1990) suggests Eisner was discussing something similar in 1979, and Pollard and Tann (1987) who have popularised the notion with regard to primary teachers more than anyone else in this country, link it to Dewey (1933) and to Stenhouse (1975).

The aim is to produce professionals who 'know in action', who can make decisions or see solutions which are apparently intuitive or non-logical but which are arrived at by skill, gained by 'reflection in action'. Schon argued against a simple techno-rationality in teaching:

> One can only develop in students a capability for reflection-in-action, but one cannot tell a student that if she/he teaches relative humidity in a certain way, one can guarantee that the pupils will learn the concept (Schon, 1983, p.68).

Pollard and Tann open their book with a four-fold summary of reflective teaching, which

> ...implies an active concern with aims and consequences, as well as with means and technical efficiency;
> ...combines enquiry and implementation skills with attitudes of open-mindedness, responsibility and wholeheartedness;
> ...is applied in a cyclical or spiralling process in which teachers continually monitor, evaluate and revise their own practice;
> ...is based on teacher judgement, informed partly by self-reflection and partly by insights from educational disciplines (1987, p.4).

There is considerable emphasis on synthesising the 'separate' domains of subject, method and theory, so that what is to be taught is analysed simultaneously with teaching method, and empirical soundings of outcomes are taken as well as active consideration of longer term effects on individuals, teaching group and society. Teachers, they suggest, must be prepared to consider the implications of their work outside the classroom and to be active in shaping educational policy, and Pollard and Tann lay considerable stress on values, perhaps lest readers think of the book solely as a 'practical' guide.

It is striking how widespread the notion of the reflective teacher has become in ITE in Britain. The term was scarcely in use in the early 1980s yet there was apparent near universal consensus about aiming for this model of the teacher in the early 1990s — 81% according to the MOTE study (Barret et al., 1992).

The notion is not without its critics, some arguing that it over-intellectualises the simple craft of teaching, and others that it has too un-political an idea of 'reflection'. It is closely linked with the idea of teaching as a profession (indeed the title 'extended professional' seems to be employed in some course documents as synonymous with reflective practitioner.) Professions are typically characterised as relatively autonomous, with restricted entry and specialised expertise, though as regards 'race' in education both Gurnah (1991) and Crozier (1991) warn that teacher professionalism has not displayed great openness. These critiques will be taken up later.

CATE, 'race' and the reflective practitioner

As regards 'race', the CATE criteria wanted 'reflective practitioners', though that is not the term it used. No-one can precisely quantify how effective it has been in encouraging institutions to produce them, but some observations are possible. In the process of gaining approval by CATE, an institution could not fail to be aware that 'race' had to be addressed in some way. Amongst the criteria for approval of courses, Circular 3/84 stated:

> Students should be prepared through their subject method work and educational studies to teach the full range of pupils they are likely to encounter in an ordinary school, with their diversity of... ethnic and cultural origins. They will need to learn how to respond flexibly to such diversity and to guard against preconceptions based on race... (DES 1984, para 11).

> ...They will also need to have a basic understanding of the type of society in which their pupils are growing up, with its racial and cultural mix... (para 12).

The composition and role of CATE was altered somewhat in 1989 but the clause cited above remained. To it was added:

> Courses should also cover other aspects of the teacher's work, including: ...the school in its wider social context, including issues of culture, gender and race... (DES 1989).

In his account of CATE's work Macintyre (1991) says the professional issues criteria (which included the one above on 'race') 'did not present CATE with significant theoretical or practical problems'. The approach adopted by many institutions in the past had been to have optional courses, and CATE found they had to insist that courses or lectures on such issues were not optional and neither should attendance be. This was apparently easily done, though unlike courses on language, for instance, hourages were never prescribed.

The upshot of these criteria was that courses in ITE had to address 'race' in some way in order to be approved by CATE, and many had done little or nothing before. Nor was CATE the only influence on ITE. In the complicated theology of approval for teacher training, the Council for National Academic Awards (CNAA) was supposed to look at the academic worth of degree proposals (except in a few colleges validated by neighbouring universities), while CATE looked at the meeting of various professional criteria by the whole college. These gods had the power of life and death so institutions tended to move with some determination to live according to the gospel. I wrote in 1987:

> Anyone who has witnessed the rite of a CNAA visit (perhaps twenty staff from other colleges, reading and questioning for two days) will know that some of this is empty ritual, but not all. HMI visits in connection with CATE accreditation contain less empty ritual, and both, if unsuccessful, require changes, replanning, rewriting, if courses are to continue. Colleges fear these visits, and course writing and the appointment (and sacrificing) of staff is affected up to two years in advance of them (Gaine, 1987; p.168).

CATE's insistence on a criterion that lecturers should have recent and relevant school experience may well have keyed in to the other Criteria, since numbers of new staff will have been recruited from urban or multi-racial schools. Insofar as this was true it produced fury among some on the Right:

> What is to stop institutions of preparation recruiting this recent practice from the worst and most politicised LEAs in the country? (O'Keeffe, 1990 p.7)

In October 1985 Keith Joseph asked CATE to look specifically at the suggestion in the newly published Swann Report that all students should 'have an opportunity of gaining some experience in a multiracial school'. According to Macintyre (1991) CATE did not press this, believing that appropriate progress was being made. He cites no evidence for this belief with regard to colleges in largely white areas where it was obviously harder to achieve, which is puzzling as he also quotes part of an HMI/CATE visit to one such college, which had two schemes for giving students experience of inner city areas:

> Many students indicated an interest in multi-ethnic education, although in a considerable number of cases their experience, knowledge and understanding were limited. In particular some students equated the issue with inner-city areas inhabited by members of ethnic minority communities. They appeared unaware of its relevance in the education of all pupils, including those living in all-white, especially rural areas such as that in which the college is situated. (Macintyre, 1991, p.156).

In practice, institutions had to show they were doing something, and for a time HMIs doing CATE scrutinies designated one of each visiting team to look at this area (among others). In the 1985 HMI report on my college there were five separate paragraphs on 'multi-cultural education', taking up about one page out of forty. During the inspection several staff were questioned about the issue, and I had to correspond with the designated HMI before the visit. The report, though positive, made a specific recommendation (setting up a resource centre) which was swiftly acted upon (DES 1987). Before the inspection a briefing day for staff was organised, at which I made a formal input and several circulars were presented. Whatever their own personal commitment to the issue, senior staff put their institutional weight behind staff being well prepared.

This did not last. Another inspection in 1989 gave far fewer signals of interest in 'race'. I was scarcely involved in the process apart from being questioned by an HMI. However, whereas in 1985 the emphasis seemed to be 'how much are you doing?', in 1989 it was more in the tone of 'justify the place of this course in the BEd'. Nevertheless, the report commented on 'multicultural' education, saying that the students' depth of understanding was 'too uneven', that students needed more confidence in applying information and insights, and that there was 'limited evidence that the policy of equal opportunities is being implemented in all specialist curriculum areas' (DES, 1990b).

In 1992 CATE was given yet another brief, a much reduced one. It also reduced the criteria for approval dramatically and removed the requirements quoted earlier. I return to this later.

Other Pressures

CATE is significant as an instrument of government policy but we have seen that it was not the only force acting on ITE establishments with regard to 'race'. At the level of national policy the CNAA was probably the most significant, validating as it did most BEds and virtually all non-university PGCEs. It had quite a strongly worded requirement for courses seeking validation from 1984, though by 1986 it had been weakened (CNAA 1984 and 1986; ARTEN 1988). Nevertheless, for the period the requirements were in operation they must have had some effect on course design, and many such courses continued into the 1990s.

Change was also brought about by the constant steady movement of teachers into ITE establishments (encouraged by CATE), bringing their current concerns with them; in multiracial areas students themselves brought their concerns back to college; in a minority of colleges black and Asian students were numerous and/or confident enough to call for change; LEA policies had some effect (particularly in colleges or polytechnics which were then financed by those LEAs); and lastly through some other policies outside of CATE at a national level (for example in the church colleges).

The Swann Report's publication in 1985 created a wave of interest and pressure for action. It brought together existing surveys and perspectives on the role of teacher training (like those of HMI) and was entirely unambiguous in its call for wider permeation and specialist courses. It also made the essential distinction between metropolitan and other areas:

> What is most immediately apparent ...apart from the general paucity of provision, is the continuing confusion of two distinct forms of provision — on the one hand, course provision designed specifically to give student teachers the particular knowledge and skills needed to teach in a multi-racial school, and, on the other hand, the preparation of all students in initial training for teaching pupils in a multi-racial society, irrespective of whether the students concerned will be teaching in an 'all-white' or multi-racial school' (p.551).

Swann successfully called upon the infant CATE to promote its concerns and supported CNAA's continuing efforts. Accepted by the Secretary of State, for a while it provided legitimation and pressure for change which was mobilised in many institutions, by HMI and CNAA. Later, as discussed in Chapter 3, it was one of the bogies identified by the Right, since its liberal tone and offical legitimation made it more of a threat than left-wing LEAs.

The ERA and after

As soon as the 1988 Education Reform Act was passed, the National Curriculum began to have an effect upon the content of ITE; whereas what was expected to be in the school curriculum before it was to some extent negotiable and variable, by the 1990s there were statutory obligations. Accordingly, there was greater expectation that ITE would produce subject expertise. This was obviously so for secondary students, but it became stressed also for the upper primary age-range. All primary students were expected to be more competent than previously in science and technology, and there was greater emphasis on assessment. In one sense this made the ITE curriculum more crowded, and it might therefore be argued that it left less space for any focus on 'race'. In practice the reduced 'space' was probably also in the priorities of ITE staff: not surprisingly, and just as in schools, the National Curriculum came to take up a great deal of anxious attention.

A guidance document issued by the NCC (NCC, 1991) includes a section headed 'Needs and Opportunities in Initial and Licensed Teacher Training — A view of the whole curriculum'. It states that newly trained teachers will need to:

— be familiar with NCC's definition of the whole curriculum and cross-curricular elements...

— consider ways in which the National Curriculum can broaden the horizon of all pupils so that they can understand and respect, learn from and contribute to the multicultural society around them;

— understand how their specialist subject(s) can contribute to the personal and social development of pupils and help prepare them for the opportunities, responsibilities and experiences of adult life;

It also suggests that initial training programmes 'might include opportunities' for student teachers to:

— discuss whole curriculum issues with tutors, teachers and peers in mixed subject as well as specialist subject groups;

— consider how LEAs and schools promote cross-curricular dimensions through whole-school policies and through the school curriculum.

It also has a chart linking NC training needs with the most recent CATE criteria, published in Circular 24/89. In the language of the NCC these are the opportunites for any mention of 'race', and potentially at least provide additional legitimation for the continued coverage of the issue.

The effect on courses

After CATE, CNAA, HMI and NCC pressure, ambiguous and general though it may be, is it possible to generalise about what ITE institutions taught students about 'race' by the beginning of the 1990s? Such generalisations would be fraught with problems, not the least of which might be re-framing the question as 'what did students learn?' We know all the colleges did something, or claimed to, because CATE required it, but there were great variations in hourages, methods of teaching, staff expertise, student receptiveness (for instance between urban PGCEs and provincial, largely white BEds), assessment and attendance requirements and local involvement. The HMI Report (DES, 1989) was optimistic, ARTEN (1988) was not, and I have anecdotal evidence of coverage being patchy (for instance, letters from students at other institutions complaining of their courses and facilities and asking for help). We can see it was on the agenda, the extent to which this was cause for celebration for some, or horror for others, remains to be seen.

'Race' in ITE in practice

I arrived in my own institution in 1985, to inherit the legacy of courses written in the late 1970s. There was a practically focused option in 'multicultural education' in year 3 of the BEd, taken by about 10-15% of students, and a further opportunity in an educational studies course later in the same year. The fact that these pre-dated requirements by CATE (indeed CATE itself) is explained by personalities. Key staff, like the co-ordinator of the BEd, had worked in a multiracial London comprehensive, and brought their experience and concerns with them. The PGCE also contained a flexible course (very common in PGCEs at the time), in this case called Contextual Studies, which allowed for brief coverage of topical themes (usually between three and six hours). Some of these were topical for one year, others, like 'race', tended to run each year.

The college is in the south east of England, in two adjacent towns, and the vast majority of students come from the Home Counties (especially those on the BEd). In common with most people in higher education, their family backgrounds could mostly be described as 'middle class', at most two percent of each annual cohort are from ethnic minorities, and 85% are female. The majority of BEd students are aged 18 or 19 and have come straight from schools or colleges but in some cohorts 30% are mature students, mainly women returners with children or people who have tried other jobs before entering ITE.

In 1985, once a new BEd was being written, it was clear from the CATE criteria that a 'race' element had to be visible, though there was no iron requirement for a discrete course. 'Permeation' was one alternative whereby the aim was for the whole curriculum to be threaded with a 'multicultural perspective'. Macintyre reports some concern at CATE over this, wondering how to ensure coverage did not remain fragmented or incomplete. Swann made the same point:

> (The)...strategy of 'permeation' may be effective where the level of awareness and commitment amongst course tutors is high, but without specific, detailed plans for compulsory input to initial courses, backed up by specialist options for those who wish to pursue the issues in more depth and widen their expertise, it may be just a paper promise (DES, 1985, p.559).

In other words, things can become so well permeated that they disappear altogether.

In 1988 the Anti-racist Teacher Education Network (ARTEN) published the outcomes of seminars and meetings it held in 1987. Its key position was that the philosophy underlying most work in ITE was multiculturalist, or as ARTEN expressed it, 'racism as an aberration, an accident resulting from an unnecessary distortion of human social relationships'. ARTEN's position was that racism had to be seen as a structural phenomenon. This was clearly some distance from the position adopted by CATE, and ARTEN notes that while questions were asked about courses (by CATE and CNAA) the questioners are not 'themselves qualified' to make judgements about courses or the people who teach them'. ARTEN argued against the likelihood of consensus within institutions if a truly anti-racist struggle was going on, since it would necessarily involve constant struggle and conflict. 'Permeation and incorporation can be seen as institutional forms of resistance' (ibid, p.5). In brief, the more an institution persuaded CATE that satisfactory, consensual permeation was taking place in a course, the more, ARTEN believed, no really challenging work was taking place.

At any event, as the person newly employed to develop 'multicultural' work, I applied the same perspective as I had done in school: students had already learned a great deal about 'race', some of it framed within a racist discourse, (see chapter one) and it did not seem very likely that permeated elements about culture in different curriculum areas were very likely to deal with inequality and teachers' possible responses. In addition I wanted to avoid the trap identified by Swann and encapsulated in this book's title: the perception that any ITE course about 'race' was about the 'inner city' and really only of interest to students planning to teach there. Here I was at an obvious starting point: I knew perfectly well the extent of racist ideas in all-white schools and the difficulty of countering them. Where better to start than with the student teachers who would for the most part be teaching in all-white primary and secondary schools?

I was relatively new to ITE, with some years' experience of A level sociology teaching and with some more recent experience of intensive anti-racist courses generally known as Racism Awareness Training (RAT). Given the considerable commitment to racial equality on the part of key senior staff (which was unusual), it was fairly easy by the autumn of 1985 to obtain agreement to compulsory one-day courses for all BEds during their first year. As I have already noted, the BEd running at that time included a third year option in 'multicultural education', taken by a minority, and a new BEd was in its very early draft stages, so these one-day courses were one way of introducing something quickly which would reach all students.

127

It is important to say something about these one-day intensives here because they coloured our later thinking and to some extent created a kind of climate among the students. They followed the style of RAT outlined in Gaine (1987), involving the key pedagogical assumptions that white people needed emotional as well as cognitive involvement to learn about racism, that this was usually a painful and challenging process, and that this personal learning was a necessary precursor to effective action as would-be teachers. It followed from these that the emotional charge might be high at times, that trainers had to be skilled and sensitive, that teaching groups had to be small (about 18) and that intensive sessions of six hours or so were more appropriate than a succession of weekly ones. There were always two trainers, one from the college and one of a group of black and Asian contacts from around the country who were keen to support this degree of commitment in ITE.

I do not want to engage in a now defunct debate about this kind of 'training', which mushroomed in local authorities for a brief period and was rapidly abandoned as a liberal sop to black demands, resulting in little more than white breast-beating and learning the right rhetoric. Whatever its weaknesses or culpability in settings like multiracial workplaces, I do not think the same criticisms apply to an institution whose purpose is teaching: it was used as a pedagogical experiment.

It stopped in 1990, not because of the results but because of increasing pressure on students' time, the difficulty of funding staff hours for elements of a BEd which were not strictly required by CATE, and the cost of paying the black and Asian trainers a fair fee (the first year or so had got by on a pittance and goodwill).

Its effects were mixed, the evaluations suggesting three issues. In the short term, the one-day courses seemed to increase interest in and a willingness to examine and challenge racist ideas and assumptions (in the students themselves or in texts and other courses). These outcomes are attested to in evaluations carried out soon after the sessions and in some cases half a term later. The anonymous returns were often very striking in their enthusiasm and self-examination.

Secondly, in the longer term, anxiety and discomfort about the issues raised seemed to surface. This became evident through myths spreading about what actually went on in the sessions ('black people just tell you how racist all white people are').

128

Thirdly, and more tentatively, the last year we ran RAT was the hardest, our impression being that the outside political climate about the 'loony left', 'race spies' and 'green sheep' (see Chapter 3) had done its work in creating a climate that was unconducive to taking racism seriously.

In the Autumn of 1988 the first cohort of a new BEd began its second year, responding to the 1983 CATE Criteria. For the first time all students had to cover issues of inequality in some depth. The CATE Criteria were met by two separate components: 'Race', Gender and Classrooms, a 30 hour course in the second year, and Education and Society in year three and year four. The reasons for the separation were a mixture of personal and logistical, to do with key individuals' main interests and the competition for students' time in the early years of a four year degree, though it also reveals something of the working assumptions of the key staff: we saw no essential problem in treating the key inequalities separately.

The first term dealt with 'race' and it was a rough ride for the staff. Most did not have first-hand knowledge of the issues concerned, so despite the recognition of the value of relatively small teaching groups and the affective-cognitive mixture of the subject matter, the course was mostly lectures to the entire group of about 100, given by myself and one or two others, with brief seminars afterwards. There was a very conscious attempt not to be too 'radical' or challenging, to take a very mild approach and to link every session firmly to classroom practicalities with which the students could identify. (For those who know the material, it may be useful to know that the first session consisted of showing Ruddell's 'Recognising Racism' programme, followed by discussion.)

To be mild and unthreatening may have been the intention, but it is not how many students received the course, and their response was occasionally a challenge but more often an apparently sullen silence. On several occasions the staff met informally after a session and exchanged their own feelings about the resistance they felt they were experiencing. As course co-ordinator I was particularly identified with the course and was undoubtedly very unpopular amongst a section of the students. Evaluations at the end of the term contained some positive feedback, but there were persistent themes about feeling accused and about bias, free speech, and 'making the problem worse by going on about it'.

The national climate was already changing into what Ball has more recently called a 'discourse of derision', although officially we were only meeting the CATE requirements. Support from senior staff in the college was unwavering, but the reactions from students and nervousness about 'starting where they were' made us tone down the course in the following year. We took the 'classrooms' in the title even more literally, cut out almost all the broader analysis, and brought in a squad of teachers for one session to give 'real' credibility. The first year RAT sessions were tailored a little to try and pre-empt this second year response, though the short-term positive reaction to them was continuing much as before.

The courses continued in this way until the 1992/3 academic year, by which time there were more staff with relevant experience and a carousel system had been evolved, one tutor repeating a 90 minute session for each of six or seven seminar groups in turn. This gave even more scope for classroom-relevant work, allowed the comparative safety of a seminar group identity to emerge (though with no fixed tutor), necessarily assumed no common sequence of sessions for the different groups and broke the close association between the content of the course and one member of staff. The seminars were on linguistic diversity; ESL strategies; teaching about native Americans; bullying and racial name-calling; assessment and achievement; the film 'A Class Divided'; and a classically 'multicultural' session about the key linguistic and religious distinctions amongst British Asians. The toning down of what we did felt like a big compromise, especially the absence of any conceptual analysis of racism, since it had certainly never been all that radical. Nevertheless, a minority of students still felt the whole course was a waste of time.

In 1992 some new data emerged. The first group to have been through RGC reached their 4th year, in which the Education and Society course contained an option on 'race', amongst others. It was the single most popular choice, chosen by almost 25% of the cohort who knew it was taught by the same person who was so closely identified with both the RAT course in their first year and RGC in their second. In individual interviews discussing reflections on RGC with this group, a common sentiment emerged: 'if it's not hurting it's not working'. In other words, though they found it uncomfortable at the time and most would not have done the course if it had been optional, by year four they had come to see it differently — they saw it as valuable enough to want to know more.

By this time I think I had become thoroughly socialised into teaching about 'race' in such a way that students were not alienated and hostile, and most responded quite positively towards the RGC course in evaluations in terms of its usefulness, the credibility of the staff, and what they perceived as the balance between 'theory' and 'practice'. As a teacher I had no wish to return to being a focus for student hostility. The evidence from the 4th years was not unambiguous, so the risk of returning to an earlier more allegedly 'confrontational' style was not taken. (It is worth stressing again that the style would not in my view be seen as confrontational by anyone who had the slightest aquaintance with anti-racist work.)

Thus by 1992 a course explicitly about 'race' and gender and another about class were established parts of the BEd. As I have indicated, not every student liked them and in the first two years of operation and indeed some hated them, but after that they were consistently evaluated positively by students and given unwavering support from senior staff.

The PGCE allowed much less time. By 1990 the Contextual Studies course had been reduced to one morning a week for a term and renamed Society, Education and Schooling. I evaluated it in 1992. There were about 90 students in all, training for first and middle schools, and secondary maths, English and history and 81 completed an evaluation form. They had various courses like the teaching of reading and how to plan their lessons (which involve some 'theory' of course) but they came to SES for what outsiders consider the real theory, the things supposedly most remote from 'real teaching' or a clear subject base. Their eleven mornings were spent on the topics of child development, 'race', special educational needs, gender, social class, drug abuse and bullying. Six tutors each specialised in one of these (one covered the last two), meeting in turn all six groups of 17 PGCEs. There were also two 'lectures', one on psychology and the teacher and the other, from a local specialist social worker, on child abuse.

The students were asked to rate each element of the course on scale of 1 = poor to 5 = excellent, and to give a separate rating for the usefulness of the session and the way it was taught. They were also asked for an overall judgement of the course on a 'too practical — too theoretical' continuum and to give a judgement of the tutors' expertise.

They liked the course. Sessions were rated for usefulness as follows, with no significant differences between age phases or subjects:

gender	3.6
'race'	3.9
social class	3.4
child development	3.5
special needs	3.7
bullying/drugs	3.6
child abuse	3.9
psychology and the teacher	3.1

They also liked the way they were taught, and attributed similar scores for methodology to those for content.

Anyone who has taught PGCE students will accept that these are high ratings: if anything, students tend to be hyper-critical and are not on the whole afraid of saying so. I doubt if students studying for first degrees would give such ratings, and if I was running a similar course for GPs or police inspectors or headteachers I would not consider these scores as grounds for closure.

On the balance of theory/practice the scores were

too practical	about right	too theoretical
3	63	15

As it happens, the majority were mature students, for the most part coming not straight from their first degrees but from years of employment (engineers, police officers, civil servants, managers, bus drivers) and/or from bringing up their own children. The average age of the group was 30 years 5 months, the youngest was 21, the oldest 51. Several were school governors.

Rising right-wing influence

By 1992 none of the evidence of what students learned from such courses seemed to matter much. We saw in Chapter 3 how a group of right-wing pressure groups and individuals mounted an increasingly successful campaign against anti-racist concerns towards the end of the 1980s. By the early 1990s they were turning their attentions towards ITE, though it had not escaped criticism earlier; in 1982 the *Daily Mail* wrote

The explosive mixture being produced in the 80s is the direct result of a second generation educated in the comprehensives over the last two decades, stimulated by well-meaning but malignant philosophies of trendy teachers coming out of training colleges with half-baked ideas on mixed ability teaching, egalitarianism, and the abolition of corporal punishment and classroom discipline (Daily Mail, 4/5/82).

In 1989 the first formal inroads were made into the 'monopoly' of institution-based ITE: the licensed and articled teacher schemes (DES Circular 18/89). The latter was a pilot school-based two-year PGCE scheme, and while it actually had almost as much college input as a one-year scheme, this was firmly limited to subject and 'method' courses, that is 'no theory'. The scheme was funded to take in only four cohorts (it proved far more expensive than the standard PGCE route). The idea of licensed teachers fits very well with the 'craft' ideas of some on the Right, discussed below. Arguably more in response to teacher shortages than right-wing pressure, it aimed to recruit non-graduates in their late twenties or older, who had some experience or skill which schools could use. The typical example given was someone with practical or scientific skills. Most of the teacher unions opposed the scheme, as did the ITE institutions, though several became involved in the brief college-based elements of the scheme. Licensed teachers were very clearly founded on an apprenticeship model, being employed by the school (usually in secondary shortage subjects) and learning on the job.

In response to the Green Paper outlining these schemes, Anthony O'Hear produced *Who Teaches the Teachers?* (Social Affairs Unit, 1988). He recommended an extension of the articled teacher route, and several measures to get influence away from LEA officials and ITE staff, partly because of what he saw as their undue concern with racial inequality.

In two earlier publications (Hillgate, 1986; Shaw, 1987) ITE was similarly mentioned as a hotbed of anti-racist subversion, but at that time there was much less attention devoted to ITE than to schooling. This began to change by 1988/9 with the first two booklets targeting ITE, and by 1992 the model CATE had been working to in the 1980s had been somewhat mauled.

Learning to Teach (Hillgate Group, 1989), developing O'Hear's points, made three criticisms of ITE. First, that it is intellectually weak:

It is difficult to think of a single department of education in a British university or polytechnic which has genuine intellectual distinction, nor is it clear what intellectual distinction in this area would really amount to (Hillgate Group, 1989, p.4).

In other words, education's claim to be an academic discipline is specious, it is essentially a low-level, practical concern, and 'educationalists' have no genuine expertise about education over and above anyone else.

Their second criticism is that it is biased, by which they mean left-wing. The critique of British society and education to be found in ITE is too influenced by Marxist sociology and a preoccupation with inequality. They cite just two course outlines from Brighton Polytechnic as examples that demonstrate their point.

Third, they argue that ITE lecturers have insufficient classroom experience. The efforts of CATE notwithstanding, the contention here is that lecturers are 'theoreticians' and removed from real classroom life. This is important as one of the foundations of their later position that teaching is a craft, and the real locus of expertise about teaching is therefore in the schools.

Another booklet critical of conventional ITE appeared in 1991, from Sheila Lawlor, the Deputy Director of the Institute for Policy Studies. *Teachers Mistaught — Training in Theories or Education in Subjects* describes itself as 'research', though the leader in the TES in the same week said that it deserved no such name. While claiming that her book is a survey of practice in PGCEs and BEds in England, Lawlor bases her comments on the prospectuses of only some of them, and makes no direct communication with the institutions at all. She comes to a series of fairly flimsy conclusions. She asserts that PGCE method work is all about current educational theory :

...practical experience has been manipulated so as to provide a vehicle for theory...

Periods of training in the classroom are chiefly regarded as providing an opportunity for putting educational theory into practice... (p.24).

The PGCE undermines the very notion of subject mastery through the relentless application of recent theory...The BEd courses, too, fail to ensure a proper knowledge of subjects and instead substitute a set of dubious theoretical assumptions to be applied at every possible instance...(p.32).

The bright graduate will be put off teaching by the emphasis on the psychological and sociological side issues... (p.40).

These assertions are somewhat sweeping and display apparent ignorance of the CATE criteria. They bear little relationship to the findings about ITE in the MOTE study published in 1992 (Barrett et al.). What Lawlor means by 'theory' is elaborated a little: it is the educational concern for inequality.

Bizarre, ill-researched, polemical, the booklet nevertheless received wide publicity. When the Secretary of State, Kenneth Clarke, announced little more than a year later an 'enquiry' into primary education, he cited Lawlor as a reference (along with Bennett (1976) and Alexander (1991)). In a speech in October 1991 Clarke stated that 'I meet too many young people who are ... put off by the length of the course. Or they go on a course and give up ... too much theory and not enough practice' (TES, 18/10/91). Eighteen months after *Teachers Mistaught* was published some sweeping changes in ITE, especially secondary PGCEs, were announced, to be followed a few months later by new primary criteria and the proposal to introduce one-year infant training and QTS for people with A levels and 'some experience' of children.

Rather reminiscent of the 'loony left' press campaigns described in Chapter 2 was the affair of 'Sharon Shrill'. Annis Garfield, a classics graduate from Cambridge resubmitted her own application for a primary PGCE (after its initial rejection) together with a fictitious one for a black woman called Sharon Shrill. The fictitious candidate had an upper second class degree including some sociolinguistics and some English (relevant for the CATE criteria) and had worked as a classroom assistant, supply teacher, playgroup leader and counsellor for young offenders. She also 'had' four grade As at A level and seven at GCSE. The real candidate had a 2:2, three unspecified pass grades at A level and five at O level, and stated in her application that 'reading was largely mistaught in schools today' and that classics is 'more relevant to the primary curriculum than any other degree'.

These details are culled from an exhaustive article in the *TES* (1991a) but they were not portrayed this way in the *Daily Mail* or on the BBC's

135

panel and phone-in 'Any Questions'. The TES suggests that Garfield became:

> ... a cause célèbre of the Right, which claims that modern teacher training methods were more sympathetic to 'left-wing, Afro-Caribbean sociologists' than to Oxbridge-educated proponents of traditional education.

The style of the coverage is less interesting than the fact that there was any coverage at all. After all, why should an individual's acceptance or not onto an ITE course be national front-page news? It seems possible at least that the same kind of network that was evidenced in Chapter 3 was once again at work, and that Ms Shrill/Garfield became a symbolic lever to bring about change. Soon afterwards the *Daily Mail* trumpeted a 'shake- up' of CATE because of the affair.

> Our education system is in turmoil. Nowhere is that more apparent than in the teacher training colleges — A shake-up of teacher training is now certainly at the top of the Government's manifesto pledges for the next election. Education Secretary Kenneth Clarke, who has condemned child-centred learning as 'silly', has not been idle. After the Sharon Shrill affair in which Cambridge classicist Annis Garfield was denied a teacher training place ... yet was offered an interview when she posed as a fictitious Afro-Caribbean feminist, he sacked some of the 'trendies' from the quango which validates teacher training courses. Further, he has ordered two enquiries: the first into the quality of courses approved, and the second into the way in which teachers are trained to teach reading. It is an open secret that he is outraged by some of the courses which have been approved (*Daily Mail*, 30/4/91).

Taylor, still the Chair of CATE after seven years, denied all this, saying that suggestions that four members had been sacked was '...offensive to dedicated volunteers who have come to the end of their office'.

It is ironic that in a chapter contributing to Graves' book (1990) Taylor comments on the climate when CATE was established:

> In many countries, there could still be found those who maintained that the only training teachers needed was effective induction into an

academic discipline, plus a spot of apprenticeship (Taylor, 1990, p.112).

Credence is given at least to the *Mail's* claims about Clarke's sympathies, however, by the fact that one of the new members of CATE was Anthony O'Hear, member of several of the right-wing think tanks, a professor of philosophy, and not obviously meeting any of the original criteria for CATE membership. The new appointments were accompanied by a letter from Clarke:

> I am sure you will be as acutely aware as I am of the extent of public interest in and concern about the quality of teacher training... I would hope that the scrutinising and monitoring of courses can be more than just a paper exercise (Clarke, 1991).

On the same day this letter was sent, the *Mail* claimed of ITE courses generally:

> Too much of their training is stuffed with sociology. They are not given enough classroom practice. And there is still too much emphasis on the fad of free expression... (*Daily Mail*, 31/1/91).

Hill (1990, 1991) argues that by 1990 ITE was being subjected to an 'ideological blitzkrieg' from the radical Right middlebrow media, the right-wing think tanks, and Conservative education ministers. He suggests their commonest themes as:

— college-based ITE should be scrapped or massively reduced;

— an apprenticeship model of training should be introduced;

— current ITE is over-concerned with changing society and with egalitarian or liberal perspectives on schooling;

— current ITE promotes multiculturalism and anti-racism;

— there is too little emphasis on classroom discipline skills;

— there is too little emphasis on knowledge and love of subject;

— there is little or no need for 'educational theory'

(derived from Hill, 1991, p.7).

There are tensions within the Right. O'Keeffe, (1990) for instance, upholds the importance of theory, and joins with other critics of government proposals in pointing out that if the practice in schools is so corrupted then placing new students there will hardly improve the situation. What he shares with the others, however, is a sense that something profoundly important about British education has been eroded or destroyed. He identifies several features of 'progressivism', but repeatedly returns to aspects of multicultural or anti-racist initiatives almost as touchstones. He does not blame teacher education for starting this, but seems to regard it as a powerful means of its reproduction.

So despite the tensions, what emerges from Hill's list above is that a central part of the Right's project must be to wrest the control of ITE away from those who currently have it.

Hill (1991) goes on to identify the range of competing perspectives on ITE in 1990s Britain. He suggests three in the centre:

'hard': exemplified by Hargreaves (1989) and Warnock (1988), whose main proposal seems to be more school-basing and a more competencies-based approach;

'soft': Plowdenite, sure of the ability of 'the profession' to do a good job if left alone;

'left/centre': Hill puts several groupings here because of the scope of their intentions. They are not, he suggests, 'overtly about the development of critical reflective transformative intellectuals'; they 'are not Radical and are not identifiably Left' (p.12).

He does not explicitly link the reflective practitioner model to this centrist grouping, but would presumably site it with the second two, at least in its most 'liberal' form. In his view a 'centre' perspective 'is the perspective of much of the current education establishment', and this would appear to be confirmed by the MOTE study (Barrett et al. 1991).

Now whereas the Right has its critique of what is, in effect, the reflective practitioner model, and believes it to be responsible through naive liberalism for the undermining of important principles in British education, the radical Left sees it as much less effective. To repeat, of the left/centre grouping, Hill says '...as it stands, its ... intentions, while laudable, are not Radical and are not identifiably left...' Whatever the Right may think.

Hill suggests a more radical stance, doubtless self-consciously proposing the Right's worst nightmare, an ITE founded upon social perspectives which emphasise social justice during economic change, egalitarianism, democratic processes and opposing sharp differentials, narrow definitions of 'standards' and elitism: teachers as, in Giroux and McLaren's phrase 'transformative intellectuals'.

The future...

As the 1990s unfold the outcome of the struggle between these perspectives seems to be as follows: the Right is increasingly able to set the ideological or at least the rhetorical agenda. They have quite effectively pilloried 'theory' in ITE and promoted a climate where school teaching is defined primarily as a skill, as a technical craft, best learned by apprenticeship giving a good grounding of subject knowledge and firm discipline. ITE is obliged to base students in school for increasing proportions of their time, acting merely as a conduit for money to schools from the Teacher Training Agency which is the body which has removed ITE from mainstream higher education funding.

Neither the reflective practitioner nor the teacher as described in the radical left model can easily survive this. Those models both require the asking of difficult questions and the standing outside taken-for-granted assumptions, so are unlikely to be achievable by individuals or small groups of students who are based in one or two schools for all of their ITE. For example, in examining teacher professionalism with regard to 'race', Gurnah (1991) notes the tendency to be self-referential and consensual, to close ranks when criticised, to honour the black professionals most like themselves, in short to 'act as minor state custodians whose practices and ideologies sustain and reproduce racial... inequalities rather than challenge them' (Gurnah, 1991, p.12).

At the moment, the economics of school-basing for primary students and the fairly concerted opposition to it from schools ensure some continuing role for ITE, but its aims are increasingly expressed as 'competencies'. Rather than (arguably) high-sounding ideals about the model of the teacher as a reflecting professional, the emphasis is increasingly on specific things a teacher must be able to do. The 1992 CATE Criteria are much briefer than those of 1984 or 1989, and are stated as a list of competencies. The requirements to cover any aspects of social inequality have gone.

In some respects the 'educational establishment' in ITE may be effecting a slippery escape from the plans of the Right, simply rewriting reflective practitioner aims and models in the language of competencies. The place of anti-racism in the ITE curriculum is much less assured. Institutions with large cores of staff with experience of anti-racist schooling may be able to avoid the dangers of invisible permeation identified by Swann, CATE and ARTEN, but my experience suggests that discrete courses are an effective minimum in most colleges. Nevertheless, in my own they have all gone. Despite the generally positive responses from students and support from senior staff, the prescribed hourages for the NC core and for school-based work have left no time for the courses undertaken by previous students, even if they were still required. The primary PGCEs no longer have even the three hours on 'race' evaluated earlier. The primary BEds initially lost their year three and four Education and Society course, then their year two course. From now on they will qualify without any time in the four years explicitly set aside to examine social inequality in general and 'race' in particular. I should stress again that no-one involved in re-writing the courses (for the third time in four years) wanted this to happen, but we were unable within the regulations to prevent it.

Ironically, in its final year of life the course regained some of its former academic bite. Partly because of the arrival of a new and well-informed member of staff and partly because, for practical reasons, we devised a different model from the practically-focused carousel. The three hour session began each week with three simultaneous lectures of an hour or so covering the same theme, with one focusing on 'race', one on class and one on gender. The themes changed from week to week: language, curriculum, assessment, the child's experience of school, separate schools, etc. After a break students reconvened in 'home group' seminars each of which had sent some of their number to each of the lectures. The seminars consisted of feedback to each other about the lectures and examining the links and connections between 'race', gender and class and, say, the curriculum. Individual students could specialise to an extent and go mostly to, say, gender lectures but everyone had to go to at least one on 'race' and class. They were assessed by group presentations half way through the term and by a written exam at the end.

Ironically in the light of the Right's objections to such things and its own subsequent demise, this was the most dramatically successful course any of the twelve staff had ever taught on. Clearly there was something about the pedagogy which worked very well, but the content was at times unashamedly theoretical, based on research literature and seldom making much reference to classroom practicalities. Students did not criticise the course for this; indeed some representatives said at a formal meeting that they would like the length doubled and a 'practical' course halved instead.

'I liked the course, it made me think, I felt it opened my eyes to all sorts of things a good teacher should be aware of.' Comments like this, of course prove that the Right is right. Impressionable, naive young minds are being indoctrinated, and it must be stopped.

Chapter 8

Local Education Authorities

A great deal has happened since a chapter with the same title was written for *No Problem Here* in 1987. So much that almost all of its suggestions and analyses are now redundant. Between 1981 and 1988/9 LEAs were increasingly involved in producing guidance about 'race' and education, developing the curriculum, formulating and promoting policies, providing in-service training and employing specialist staff. Since the passing of the Education Reform Act in 1988 their advice role changed to inspection and was further diminished by a later Act which established Ofsted. The ability of LEAs to promote policy has been diminished in proportion to the delegation of funds to schools, as has their employment of specialist staff centrally. The priorities for in-service work are set by the schools largely in response to the government's National Curriculum, in the confines of which any development work has to take place. LEAs have lost control of polytechnics, colleges of higher education, further education colleges, and whatever proportion of their schools have become grant maintained. At the time of writing they are grappling with labyrinthine funding formulae which seem to be designed to maintain the differential between LEA and GMS schools, and their complete demise is being mooted by the creation of 'single tier' district councils.

An NFER study by Taylor in 1992, using local advisers/inspectors as respondents showed that at least one fifth had serious concerns about the future of multicultural/anti-racist work. Respondents in county LEAs cited the absence of any lead from the DES or the NCC; reduced funding; restructuring of LEA services; the 'no problem here' syndrome at all levels, but especially in 'mostly white' schools' (p.6); indifference; the level of awareness of the increasingly powerful school governors; reduced ability to mount inset and marginalisation because of other changes.

LEAs achieved mythic status for the policy makers of the late 1980s, as apparent dens of all they most disliked but actually as centres of power they could not control. They had to be demonised into Bogey Brent, Harpie Haringey and Evil ILEA to make self- evident the need for schools to opt out of their tormenting, doctrinaire control. Chapter three tries to show how much this was 'hyped', but it did much to legitimate the diminution of their powers.

In the light of all this, it is worth briefly recording what LEAs achieved in promoting racial equality, especially 'shire' LEAs.

As mentioned briefly in chapter three, there were several significant outcomes of the Swann Report in largely white LEAs. The most direct outcomes were the establishment of centrally funded 'white areas' development work through staffed projects and in-service courses. The Report also increased the impetus to appoint specialist advisers/inspectors in the field, and many LEAs moved towards evolving their own policies.

The staffed projects were funded under the Education Support Grants (ESG) scheme, in which LEAs received 70% of the salaries for schemes, which could last up to five years. Central funding signified ESGs were central policy, their varying implementation was the responsibility of the LEAs who were awarded the money.

At this early stage the distinction between ESG and Section 11 funding was not clear to many LEAs and many early bids were unsuccessful. Those which were successful dealt mainly with multiracial areas or multiracial schools: the focus was still on black and Asian children. By 1986, however, the message of Swann had penetrated more clearly, and HMIs were concerned to encourage 'white' LEAs to make ESG bids. By 1988 almost all LEAs in England had mounted an ESG project (119 in all) in this field, lasting from between one to five years, the majority being focused on white areas. The last ones 'expired' in 1993, since after 1988 the issue was removed from the list of national priorities and replaced by the National Curriculum following the Education Reform Act.

Tomlinson and Coulson (1988 and 1990) surveyed 23 of the projects which particularly focused on white areas, visiting their sample projects and compiling questionnaire data. They found that the working strategies of the projects varied widely. Some were not in schools at all, being sited instead in FE colleges, careers or library services. Those which were school-focused sometimes had a huge brief of working in any schools which requested them, while others had a pyramid of secondary and primary schools and still others had a more manageable group of self-selected schools, sometimes all in one phase.

Evaluation of the effect of these projects is problematic. The DES required less of them in this respect than of some other prioritised areas, and, apart from an HMI conference in 1988, made no attempt to disseminate their work. The separate LEA projects were only linked with each other in a very ad hoc way, and never by DES or HMI design. The NAME conference in 1987 organised an initial meeting (Gaine and Pearce, 1988) which developed into a more formal network with a newsletter and a series of national meetings in 1987, 1988 and 1989. After this initial contact between projects was brought about by NAME it was maintained by the workers themselves. At least one formal evaluation of a primary schools project was conducted by one of the ESG workers (Epstein, 1991 unpublished, and partly in Epstein, 1993). Many of Taylor's adviser respondents reported that these projects had improved the situation considerably, though as all the projects have closed since the study was completed in 1991 we cannot judge their continuing effect in the mid-nineties.

It is nevertheless reasonable to believe that the projects have had some effect. Tomlinson (1990) estimates that 4,000 teachers have been directly involved with them, and that many of these teachers did not see their involvement and development as temporary. Epstein's more localised study claims significant changes in practice in the Project schools. Publications have also emerged: practical handbooks for teachers from Wiltshire (White, 1988); Cumbria (Brown et al 1990); Birmingham (Epstein and Sealey, 1990); Warwickshire (Farrell, 1991); Northamptonshire (Thorp, 1992) and Hampshire (Hix, 1992) and more reflective books from Dorset (Naidoo, 1992), Hampshire (Massey, 1990) and Birmingham (Epstein, 1993); articles from Warwickshire (Sharma, 1987); Hampshire

(Massey, 1987); Cumbria (Brown, 1988) and Leicestershire (Chauhan, 1988). In some authorities the claim is made that the philosophy and the funding have been effectively 'mainstreamed', so that the pump-priming purpose of the grants scheme has been realised. In other authorities (like Hampshire) keeping the stock of a resources centre up to date ensures continued material assistance to teachers after the funding for staff ended. Other effects, if there are any, will be more subtle changes in teachers' perceptions and attitudes.

'Education for ethnic diversity' was removed from the list of priority areas in 1988 and replaced by the National Curriculum. To suggest that this was a simple substitution is to oversimplify. It cannot be assumed that the ESGs demonstrated particular local commitment — the bulk of the funds, after all, came from central government, and most of the shire counties which applied for ESG grants were controlled by the same Conservative Party which was by the late 1980s moving inexorably to the right in education policy. Or maybe it was not the same Conservative Party, since several shire Tories have openly criticised what they see as the dogmatic policy shift at the centre.

It is unclear how the work of the ESGs will be continued, if it all, and this was certainly a concern expressed by the project workers interviewed by Poulson and Tomlinson. The 'mainstreaming' of the issue and hence the funding aimed at by Warwickshire, Derbyshire and others was eroded in 1990 and subsequent years by Poll Tax capping, general cuts, a change in Section 11 regulations (now prohibiting any general multicultural/ anti-racist work) and the attrition of LEA influence through Local Management of Schools and other measures.

Another specific 'white areas' development born of Swann was the prioritising of 'multicultural issues' in Circular 1/86, which again provided central funds for development work in white areas, this time for 20 day courses for teachers. (Although when contributing to several of these courses in the south of England, I noticed that, despite the declared intention, teachers from multiracial schools in otherwise largely white LEAs were much in evidence.) These courses were to be based regionally in higher education establishments, so Berkshire, Buckinghamshire and northern Hampshire used Bulmershe; Wiltshire, Gloucestershire and Avon used St Paul's and St Mary's at Cheltenham; Kent and East Sussex used Christ Church, Canterbury; West Sussex, Dorset and southern

Hampshire used Southampton University and Warwickshire used the University of Warwick. Though legitimised and hence funded after Swann, some of these courses built upon work already being carried out by innovators: Oxfordshire had a multicultural education adviser in 1982, Taylor and Mortimer were mounting courses in Devon in the early 1980s (Taylor, 1984). The National Union of Teachers was also active in promoting anti-racist training from late 1982 (NUT, 1983).

Most of the courses focused on secondary schools, and some aimed to recruit two teachers from each school, and preferably senior ones, so that real developments were initiated. No systematic follow-up on a national scale has been undertaken on these courses to see what effect they might have had, though some evaluated themselves to an extent. They remained on the priority list for 2 years, though some ran for longer than that (indeed one was still running, heavily disguised, in 1993) and thus each influenced cohorts of at least forty or so, some considerably more. We cannot know the extent of this influence or how it has spread, though the number of in-service days in the schools represented on courses has been considerable. In Hampshire, 'Multicultural Support Groups' were established for those who had done the Southampton course, but by 1990 none of these seemed to be still functioning.

The other white areas development worth noting was the appointment of advisers or inspectors and officers in largely white LEAs. This was formally recommended by Swann, and widely taken up. The appointments to some extent overlapped with the adopting of policies in white LEAs during the mid to late 1980s. By 1989 the majority of English LEAs had a policy of some kind (though as Mullard pointed out in 1983, 'policies' are not always backed by a vote of LEA elected members). In some LEAs, such as Hampshire and Hertfordshire, advisers were appointed when the policy was in a draft form and their first task was to finalise it.

These appointments could be seen as tokenistic gestures. Certainly the advisers in shire counties had an impossible cross-phase, cross-subject brief compared to many of their more specialised colleagues, and they may well have been additionally responsible for whatever ESL and Section 11 work was done in the county. However, though it is as difficult to evaluate their effect as it is that of the ESG workers, it would be hard to argue that they have had no effect at all. They were at least symbolic of some kind of understanding that there was an educational issue to address. To that extent, at least, they represented a change, since their appointment would have been inconceivable in the 1970s. It remains to be seen whether the reduction of central LEA influence and funding and LEA restructuring as a result of the 1988 Education Reform Act leads to the redeployment of such staff, or to their non-replacement when they leave. This seems almost inevitable (there was not a single advertisement for such a post in the 1993/4 school year).

There is anecdotal evidence of another factor at work in individual schools and sometimes in LEAs: the movement of staff from multiracial areas. Schools in Hampshire, Dorset and Sussex appoint senior staff from Brent, Bristol and inner London, and the same must be true of many shire counties. While not all necessarily bring significant new insights, many clearly do. In some cases, the language and assumptions imbibed in urban areas where 'race' was indisputably an issue may ensure a sympathetic support for ESG workers, in-service courses, close attention to this 'dimension' of the National Curriculum, or produce a more informed response to the needs of isolated black pupils.

Lastly, what of the policies which most counties, including the shires, had by 1988? To my knowledge none have rescinded them (though Berkshire thought about it, see Gaine, 1989). Taylor (1992) reports that there are as many LEAs revising policies as there are with 'stable' ones, though the nature of the revisions is not clear: some are reducing their scope and others are rewriting them into, for instance, general equal opportunities policies. About 20 LEAs have developed policies since the ERA, though this is more likely to be locally motivated than inspired by the Act itself. Some pre-ERA policies clearly live on: Hampshire, Hertfordshire and Northamptonshire all have harassment guidelines which require monitoring as part of their policies and indeed Northamptonshire markets an in-service pack on racial harassment. Taylor notes a small growth in guidelines about ethnic monitoring, bilingualism and Travellers. Whatever the growth, however, a reasonably strict definition of a policy is something which actually converts principles into resources, and since LEAs have fewer resources it follows that the policies cannot be the forces they once were.

My largely impressionistic conclusion is that after ten years of various influences and developments — ESGs, policies, specialist staff, specialist courses, publications, the effect of Swann — there is a different, better, climate about 'race' in many white areas. In 1992 two thirds of Taylor's respondents in county LEAs felt some progress was still being made, though few saw the ERA as helpful and most saw the national climate as unpropitious.

Since the capacity of LEAs to create their own climate is much reduced, it may no longer make much sense to speak of differences between them, but it is not too naive to hope that there are many individual schools all over England, and concentrations in the former spheres of influence of some LEAs, where there is much less of an attitude of 'no problem here'. There is no point in being glibly optimistic, but we should not forget the work that has been done nor assume that the Right has destroyed it all.

Changing the Curriculum: Sources

This is intended to be a brief guide of what to read for ideas and practical suggestions. Case studies of work in particular settings are referred to in chapters one, four and five, in-service training manuals and handbooks are listed at the end of chapter seven, academic references are in the bibliography.

This section is divided into:

really practical handbooks;

general works with useful ideas and arguments;

bibliographies and guidelines for selection of materials;

a few classroom materials directly focusing on 'race' and racism.

There is a convincing argument that no teacher will use these materials and suggestions well unless they have examined their own preconceptions about 'race'. The same probably goes for their assumptions about inequality more generally and about pedagogy too. Be warned!

Practical handbooks written with white areas in mind

ARKELL, T. (1988) *Irish Cultural Studies: A Teaching Pack.* Trentham Books
Useful anywhere in the country and aimed at the upper junior/lower secondary age-range, this could provide an interesting alternative or complement to consideration of any other minorities.

ANTONOURIS, G. and WILSON, J. (1989) *Equal Opportunities in Schools: New Dimensions in Topic Work,* Cassell
A book for primary schools which provides a careful rationale about teaching topics and then works through some examples, which are backed up by a very good collection of specific sources for teachers and pupils. Published just after the Education Reform Act so makes no reference to the National Curriculum, but the suggestions are still usable.

BROWN, C, BARNFIELD, J and STONE, M, (1990) *A Spanner in the Works,* Trentham
Developed and trialled by the ESG team in infant and junior schools in Cumbria (see chapter 3). Each of the thirty three chapters is a concrete suggestion, almost all of them directly curricular, and each one states the age-range and type of school/s it was developed in.

DABYDEEN, D (1988) *A Handbook for Teaching Caribbean Literature,* Heinemann
This really is a handbook, with contributions from people who know particular authors' work well and how to work with it in school.

DEVELOPMENT EDUCATION CENTRE (1991) *Theme Work, A Global Perspective in the Primary Curriculum in the '90s,* Birmingham DEC
Developed by a large team of teachers in Birmingham. Apart from sections about planning theme work and children working together, this contains four detailed examples: what is a country? roots and journeys; images and change.

DODD, P. *Mathematics From Around the World* (2 books) Self-published, available from Manchester Development Education Project, 810 Wilmslow Road, Didsbury, Manchester M20 2QR.

EPSTEIN, D. and SEALEY, A. (1990) *Where it Really Matters,* Birmingham DEC
From the Birmingham 'white areas' ESG project and aimed at junior schools, this book places racism at the centre of its concerns and works through different aspects of a school's work. It gives overall guidance and suggestions rather than more narrowed-down lesson or topic ideas, but is concise enough to serve as all a teacher needs to start considering and putting anti-racism into practice.

FARRELL, P. (1990) *Multicultural Education*, Scholastic Publications
Also the product of an ESG project, this time Warwickshire's. This is exceptionally accessibly written with a very unthreatening introduction, neatly leading into quite a searching in-service activity for staff. It has suggestions for development in all subjects with useful lists of materials, too, as well as tackling some whole-school issues. Aimed at primary schools.

FISHER, S. and HICKS, D. (1986) *World Studies 8-13, A Teacher's Handbook*
Not solely about 'race' by any means, but firmly grounded in a philosophy which values fairness and justice. Lots of useable strategies.

GOODY, J. (ed.) (1992) *Multicultural Perspectives in the English Curriculum*, available from National Association for the Teaching of English
Useful articles and specific suggestions about literature.

GREGORY, A. and WOOLARD, N. (1988) *Looking into Language: Diversity in the Classroom*, Trentham (out of print)
Not really written with white areas in mind but an excellent classroom manual. Like the ILEA book below, invaluable to anyone wanting to explore language diversity whether or not such diversity is present in the class.

GUNNER, L. (1984) *A Handbook for Teaching African Literature*, Heinemann
Goes through several key books and authors with practical suggestions and useful background.

HADDOCK, L. and COHEN, P. (1994) *Anansi Meets Spiderwoman: 8-14 curriculum resources for tackling common sense racism in pupil cultures*, Cultural Studies Project, University of London Institute of Education
This is the same Phil Cohen mentioned in chapter 4, using cultural studies to explore the complexity of positions children live with and construct every day. The materials were trialled in Southwark schools and contain many useful process comments and reflections.

HESSARI, R. and HILL, D. (1989) *Practical Ideas for Multicultural Learning and Teaching in the Primary Classroom*, Routledge
Written on the basis of Ruth Hessari's work in East Sussex, this is grounded in experience of doing, in mainly white classes, what she recommends to others. Racism is not explicitly raised in her examples, but there is an important section on work about self-esteem in white children: '...one of the bedrocks of a personality that is secure enough to embrace variety and change is good self-esteem' (p.118).

HICKS, D. and STEINER, M. (1989) *Making Global Connections: a World Studies Workbook*, Oliver and Boyd
Like all world studies materials, good for methods and for broadening viewpoints.

HILLARY, M. (1991) *The Hampshire Development Education 14-16 Project*, Hampshire Development Education Centre
A report of a year's work in internationalising the curriculum. Brief examples from different schools and ages are given, on a subject by subject basis.

HIX, P (1992) *Kaleidoscope: Themes and Activities for Developing the Multicultural Dimension in the Primary School*, Southgate/Hampshire County Council
Yet another product of an ESG white areas project, this contains advice and experience about six themes — ourselves, food, communication, shelter, sacred places and journeys — based on thorough trialling in Hampshire schools. Twinning with multiracial schools is a theme which runs through the book, thereby imparting a good deal of useful advice. Tasks and ideas are related to National Curriculum ATs and Programmes of Study, though many of these have now changed.

ILEA ENGLISH CENTRE, (1981) *The Languages Book*, ILEA (now distributed by Harcourt Brace Jovanovich).
Do not be put off by the date, it still has many useful, practical ideas, though not all of them about 'race' and not all of them immediately useable in a monolingual classroom.

KRAUSE, M. (1983) *Multicultural Mathematics Materials*, Jonathan Press
American, so not always easy to get, but good and practical.

LAMONT, G. and BURN, S. (1994) *Initial Guidelines for Values and Visions: Spiritual Development and Global Awareness in the Primary School*, Manchester Development Education Project
Sets out principles and has lots of workable suggestions and strategies.

MANTRA (1991) *Mathematics Around the World*, MANTRA
Aimed at primary schools and very practical.

PEACOCK, A. (Ed) (1991) *Science in Primary Schools: the Multicultural Dimension*, Macmillan Education
Closely linked to National Curriculum Science.

PRUTZMAN, P. *et al* (1988), *The Friendly Classroom for a Small Planet*, New Society Publishers (Santa Cruz)
Not directly about 'race', but contains some exercises encouraging co-operation and dealing with conflict, useful if you are going to examine contentious issues.

ROWE, D. and NEWTON, J. (1994) *You, Me Us: Social and Moral Responsibility for Primary Schools*, Citizenship Foundation/Home Office
This contains only a brief section about 'race' (in a larger one called Respecting Differences) and the whole publication rather assumes citizenship 'lessons' rather than weaving ideas about justice into the rest of the curriculum, but it carries heavy legitimacy (endorsements in the front from the Secretary of State for Education and the Home Secretary) and even suggests teachers try a modified version of the blue eyes/brown eyes simulation (see p.113).

RUNNYMEDE TRUST (1993) *Equality Assurance and the School Curriculum*, Runnymede/Trentham Books
Comprehensive guidance on racial equality and the National Curriculum, produced to fill the gap left by the NCC. Written by an experienced group of anti-racist educators, it contains a kind of 'performance indicators' list for every subject, suggestions for each key stage, and guidelines for whole-school issues.

SHAN, S. and BAILEY, P. (1991) *Multiple Factors: Classroom Mathematics for Equality and Justice*, Trentham
The title says it all, and it delivers just what it promises. Lively, stimulating, packed with useable examples and well informed, of use in any school.

SUPPLE, C. (1993) *From Prejudice to Genocide: Learning About the Holocaust*, Trentham
A powerful book, thoroughly researched and packed with teaching ideas.

THORP, S., DESHPANDE, P. and EDWARDS, C. (1994) *Race Equality and Science Teaching*, Association for Science Education
Like its companion in-service book, I have seen this snapped up on sight by teachers. Well researched and thorough, it presents realistic examples which primary and secondary teachers can use. It also argues authoritatively that science cannot be seen as a culture-free activity.

VITAL LINK LTD, (1999) *Invisible Victorians*, Vital Link (also Tudor and Stuart Times; Benin, Art and Society).

WHITE, N, (1987), *Mathematics for All*, Wiltshire ESG Project, Wilton Middle School, Salisbury
The last in this list from an ESG project, though one of the first ones produced. It is accessible and has immediate usefulness to any teacher who teaches maths.

WOOD, A. with Oxley, J., Prior, I., Sims, P. (1995) *Homing In, A Practical Resource for Religious Education in Primary Schools*, Trentham, forthcoming.
How to make, understand and use artefacts from Christianity, Islam, Hinduism, Judiasm and Sikhism.

WOOD, A. and RICHARDSON, R. (1993) *Inside Stories: wisdom and hope for changing worlds*, Trentham
Traditional tales from many cultures, with practical suggestions for use.

Journal

Multicultural Teaching, Trentham Books, Westview House, 734 London Rd., Oakhill, Stoke on Trent ST4 5NP
This is certainly the best for practising teachers, at least make sure your local teacher education establishment and teachers' centre subscribe.

General Curriculum Advisory texts (not usually written with white areas particularly in mind)

ALTARF, (1984) *Challenging Racism*, ALTARF
Lots of case studies, clearly reflecting their London base.

ARORA, R. and DUNCAN, C. (eds.), (1986) *Multicultural Education, Towards Good Practice*, Routledge
Useful individual chapters on art, humanities, maths and science.

BRANDT, G. (1986) *The Realisation of Anti-racist Teaching*, Falmer
Rather a misleading title, as most of the book consists of a (good) discussion of what anti-racist education ought to be. The classroom observations make up quite a small part at the end.

COLE, M. (Ed) 1989 *Education for Equality*, Routledge
Many useful chapters by practitioners.

CRAFT, M. and BARDELL, G. (Eds), (1984) *Curriculum Opportunities in a Multicultural Society*, Harper Education
Focuses on secondary history, geography, social science, RE, English, PE, dance, modern languages, maths, chemistry, biology, art and design and home economics. As the subjects reveal, it was compiled before the National Curriculum was even thought of.

EYTARN, (1994) *Focus on Equality*, Early Years Trainers Anti- racist Network.
Compilation of articles of special interest to those who work with young children.

EYTARN, (1992) *All Our Children*, EYTARN
Aimed at the early years, information on racism and travellers, as well as on sexism and disability.

HOULTON, D. (1986) *Cultural Diversity in the Primary School*, Batsford
Rather a densely written book, though it contains lots of discussion and arguments based upon a sound knowledge of primary schools.

KING, A. and REISS, M. (1993), *The Multicultural Dimension of the National Curriculum*, Falmer
Subject by subject suggestions for the National Curriculum, of varying immediacy for teachers. The less immediate ones are nevertheless interesting, often recounting the sagas and battles in the NC's formation.

KLEIN, G. (1993) *Education Towards Race Equality*, Cassell
A clear overview of past debates and current issues and possibilities.

MASON, R (1988) *Art Education and Multiculturalism*, Croom Helm

NATIONAL ASSOCIATION OF HEAD TEACHERS, (1994) *Managing Equality*, NAHT

NELSON, N. *et al* (1994) *Multicultural Mathematics*, Oxford University Press
Some theoretical arguments as well as useable classroom examples.

OSLER, A. (Ed) (1994) *Development Education: Global Perspectives in the Curriculum*, Cassell
A compilation of some very experienced practitioners, with an excellent resources section.

PETERS, W. (1987) *A Class Divided*, Yale University Press
A written account of the blue eyes/brown eyes simulation mentioned in chapters 4 and 6.

REISS, M. (1993) *Science Education for a Pluralist Society*, Open University Press

ROSE, D (1992) *Home, School and Faith*, David Fulton/Roehampton Institute

SCAA (1994) *Glossary of Terms in Religious Education*, SCAA

SCAFE, S (1989) *Teaching Black Literature*, Virago
Takes a clear position rather than being a straightforward manual — makes you think.

SIRAJ-BLATCHFORD, I (1994) *The Early Years*, Trentham
Accessible and clear, this is a useful confidence-building book for teachers wondering how to deal with racism in the early years.

SHAP, (Annually) *Calendar of Religious Festivals*, SHAP

STRAKER-WELDS, M. (ed.), (1984) *Education for a Multicultural Society*, Case studies in ILEA Schools, Bell and Hyman
So much of the context has changed, in ILEA as well as the curriculum, this does not have a lot to offer those in white areas today, though the maths chapter may do.

TWITCHIN, J and DEMUTH, C, (1985) *Multicultural Education*, BBC
Lots to think about, lots of case studies.

Compilations of resources, annotated fiction bibliographies, books about stereotyping and learning materials

Note: excellent sources of new and inexpensive guides and teaching materials are the several Development Education Centres around the country. They often focus on equality issues and disseminate ideas which are tried and tested in classrooms, across all areas of the curriculum. They provide frequently updated lists of what is available, and are very are efficient with orders.... Here are some addresses

Centre for Global Education, University of York, Heslington, YO1 5DD

Commonwealth Institute, 230 Kensington High Street, London W8 6NQ

Development Education Centre, 998 Bristol Rd, Selly Oak, Birmingham, B29 6LE

Development Education Dispatches Unit, 151-3 Cardigan Road, Leeds, LS6 1LT

Development Education Project, 810 Wilmslow Road, Didsbury, Manchester M20 20R

Intermediate Technology Group, Myson House, Railway Terrace, Rugby, Warwickshire, CV21 3HT

OXFAM Education Department, 274 Banbury Road, Oxford, OX2 7DZ (also regional education offices in many big cities).

BROOKING, S., FOSTER, M. and SMITH, S. (19873 *Teaching for Equality,* Runnymede Trust

DIXON, B. (1977) *Catching Them Young: Sex, Race and Class in Children's Fiction*, Pluto

DIXON, B. (1982) *Now Read On — Recommended Fiction for Young People*, Pluto

DIXON, B. (1989) *Playing Them False: a Study of Children's Games, Toys and Puzzles*, Trentham

Extending his older work on children's fiction, this examines the kind of criteria we ought to consider when buying playthings and learning materials for younger children.

ELKIN, J. and TRIGGS, P. (1986) *Books for Keeps Guides to Children's Books for a Multicultural Society*, (0-7 and 8-12), Books for Keeps

GUPTARA, P. (1986) *British Black Literature*, Dangaroo Press
Using a very inclusive definition of 'black', this contains everything from details of black anti-slavery campaigners writing in Britain in the 1800s to novels privately published in Delhi.

ILEA, (1985) *Everyone Counts*, ILEA Learning Resources (now distributed by Harcourt Brace Jovanovich)
Deals with stereotyping in mathematics materials.

KLEIN, G. (1985) *Reading Into Racism*, Routledge and Kegan Paul

MILNER, D. (1983) *Children and Race, 10 Years On*, Ward Lock
Readable and well researched, useful background for anyone concerned about pupils' attitudes.

OXFORD DEC, (1992) *Books to Break Barriers, A Review Guide of Multicultural Fiction for Young People*, Oxford Development Education Centre
Starts with pre-school readers and goes up to 14-18 year olds; separate section on poetry.

PLAY MATTERS (1989) *Play for All*, Play Matters/Lancashire MEG Support Service

PRIESWERK, R. (ed.), (1980) *The Slant of the Pen: Racism in Children's Books*, World Council of Churches

STINTON, J. (Ed) (1981) *Racism and Sexism in Children's Books*, (ed.), Writers and Readers

WGARCR (1991) *Guidelines for the Selection and Evaluation of Child Development Books*, Working Group Against Racism in Children's Resources

WGARCR (1992) *Guidelines for the evaluation and selection of toys and other resources for children*, WGARCR

WGARCR (1993), *Guidelines and Selected Titles: 100 Picture Books*. WGARC.

ZIMET, S. G. (1976) *Print and Prejudice*, Sara Goodman Zimet, Hodder and Stoughton

Classroom materials on 'race' and racism

ATTEWELL, A. and WALKER, S. (1992) *Mary Seacole: teacher's pack and learning resource*, Black Cultural Archives/Florence Nightingale Museum

BIRMINGHAM EDUCATION (1990) *Famous Black People Posters*, Section XI Pupil Support Project, Balden Road, Birmingham B32 2EH

BYGOTT, D. (1992) *Black and British*, Oxford

CLEGG, J (1994) *Fu Manchu and the 'Yellow Peril': the Making of a Racist Myth*, Trentham

EYTARN, (1994) *Combating Racial Prejudice Against Irish People*, EYTARN

EYTARN, (1994) *Combating Racial Prejudice Against Jewish People*, Early Years Trainers Anti-Racist Network (PO Box 28, Wallasey, L45 9NP)

FILE, N., and POWER, C. (1981), *Black Settlers in Britain*, Nigel File and Chris Power, Heinemann

GREENWICH, (1993) *Racetracks: A Resources Pack for Tackling Racism with Young People*, Equalities Unit, Borough of Greenwich

HOSKING, T. (1984) *Black People in Britain 1650-1850*, MacMillan

ILEA (1978) *India, World History Outlines* (also available on China) ILEA (now distributed by Harcourt, Brace Jovanovich)

INSTITUTE of RACE RELATIONS, (1982/4/6), *Roots of Racism, Patterns of Racism, How Racism Came to Britain* and *The Fight Against Racism*, Institute of Race Relations

KILLINGRAY, D. (1987) *The Transatlantic Slave Trade*, Batsford

de la MOTHE, G. (1993) *Reconstructing the Black Image*, Trentham

SHERWOOD, M. (1993) *Black Peoples in the Americas*, Savannah Press

TUCKER, J. (1993) *Britain and the Black Peoples of the Americas 1550-1930*, Jet Publications

TWELLS, A. (1992) *The Empire in South Yorkshire 1700-1860*, South Yorkshire Development Education Centre (Aimed at KS3)

USPG (1975) *The Testimony of Chief Seattle*, tape/slide, United Society for the Propagation of the Gospel
A remarkable speech from the 1800s by a Native American chief, spoken by an actor with accompanying slides. Makes many multicultural, anti-racist and environmental points.

Bibliography

In the main, these are works referred to in the text as distinct from handbooks and sourcebooks for teachers with a clear curriculum focus, which are listed separately. Such books referred to in the text are not usually listed twice.

ALTARF (1984) Challenging Racism, ALTARF

Alhibai, Y (1987) The Child Racists, New Society, 4.12.87

Akhtar, S (1986) They Call Me Blacky, TES, 19.9.86

AMMA (1988) Our Multicultural Society, the Educational Response, Assistant Masters and Mistresses Association

Amory, M (1988) The Need for Anti-racist Education Policies in All-white Areas, Speech to 1987 NAME conference, in Gaine and Pearce (1988)

Amory, M (1987) How They Brought the Bad News to Brent, Guardian 28/4/87

Anderson, B (1989) Antiracism and Education — Strategies for the 1990s, Multicultural Teaching Vol 7 No 3.

Arora, R, and Duncan, C (eds.) (1986) Multicultural Education, Towards Good Practice, Routledge

ARTEN (1987) Occasional Papers 1, 2 and 3, Jordanhill College

ARTEN (1988) Permeation: The Road to Nowhere, ARTEN Occasional Paper 4, Jordanhill College

Bacal, A (1991) Ethnicity in the Social Sciences, Paper in Ethnic Relations No 3, Centre for Research in Ethnic Relations, Warwick university.

Bagley, C and Verma, G (1972) Some Effects of teaching designed to promote understanding of racial issues in adolescence, Journal of Moral Education vol 1, no 3.

161

Ball, S (1984) Comprehensive Schooling, a Reader, Falmer

Bansal, R 1990, A Sikh by Night, TES, 20.7.90

Banton, M (1987) The Battle of the Name, New Community Vol XIV, No 1/2, Autumn 1987

Barker, M (1981) The New Racism, Junction Books

Barrett, E (with Barton, Furlong, Galvin, Miles and Whitty) (1992) Initial Teacher Education in England and Wales: A Topography, Modes of Teacher Education Research Project.

Bennett, N (1976) Teaching Styles and Pupil Progress, Open Books

Berkshire, (1983) A Policy for Racial Equality, Royal County of Berkshire

Bowker, G (1968) The Education of Coloured Immigrants, Longman

Braham, Peter; Rattansi Ali and Skellington, Richard (1992) Racism and Anti-racism, Sage

Brandt, G (1986) The Realisation of Anti-Racist Teaching, Falmer

Brown, C (1985) Black and White Britain, Gower/Policy Studies Institute

Brown, C and Gay, P (1985) Racial Discrimination 17 years after the Act, PSI

Brown, C (1988) The White Highlands: Anti-racism, Multicultural Teaching vol 6, no. 2, pp 38-9

Cashmore, E (1982) Black Sportsmen, Routledge and Kegan Paul

Cashmore, E (1987) The Logic of Racism, Allen and Unwin

Centre for Contemporary Cultural Studies, (1982) The Empire Strikes Back, Hutchinson

Chauhan, C (1988) Anti-racist teaching in white areas, a black perspective, Multicultural Teaching vol 6, no. 2, pp 35-7

Clarke, K (1991) Letter to Sir William Taylor, Chair of CATE, 31st January

Clarke, K (1992) Speech for the Northern of England Education Conference, 4th Jan. Conservative Central Office

Coard, B (1971) How the West Indian Child is made Educationally Sub-normal in the British School System, New Beacon Books

Cohen, G (with Bosanquet, Ryan, Parekh, Keegan and Gress) (1986) The New Right, Runnymede Trust

Cohen, P (1992) It's Racism What Dunnit, in Donald and Rattansi, (1992)

Commission for Racial Equality, (1981) Racial Harassment on London Housing Estates, CRE

Commission for Racial Equality, (1984) Why Keep Ethnic Records? CRE

Commission for Racial Equality, (1985) Suspensions in Birmingham Schools, CRE

Commission for Racial Equality, (1988a) Medical School Admissions, CRE

Commission for Racial Equality, (1988b) Learning in Terror, CRE

Commission for Racial Equality (1992) Response to DES Consultation on Proposals for Reform of Initial Teacher Training, CRE

Council for National Academic Awards (1984) Multicultural Education Discussion Paper (Ref 2f/17) CNAA

Craft, M, (Ed) (1981) Teaching in a Multicultural Society — the Task for Teacher Education, Falmer

Craft, A and Bardell, G (Eds) (1984) Curriculum Opportunities in a Multicultural Society, Harper Education

Craft, M (1982) Education for Diversity, University of Nottingham School of Education

Craft, M (1984) Education and Cultural Pluralism, Falmer

Crozier, G. (1991) Some contradictions between teachers' professionalism and antiracist education, Multicultural Teaching Vol. 9 No. 3, Summer 1991

Daily Mail (1991a) Who Will Teach the Teachers? 31st January

Daily Mail (1991b) Forget the theory, just teach us to teach, 30th April

Daniel, W (1968) Racial Discrimination in England, Penguin

Davies, A-M, Holland, J, and Minhas, R, (1990) Equal Opportunities in the New ERA, Hillcole Group

Department of Education and Science, (1963) Robbins Report, HMSO

Department of Education and Science, (1967) Children and Their Primary Schools (The Plowden Report) DES/HMSO

Department of Education and Science, (1977) Education in Schools, HMSO

Department of Education and Science, (1980) HM Inspection to Investigate the Coverage of Multicultural Education in Teacher Training Courses, HMSO

Department of Education and Science (1981) West Indian Children in Our Schools (The Rampton Report) HMSO Cmnd 8273

Department of Education and Science (1984) Circular No 3/84, Initial Teacher Training: Approval of Courses, HMSO

Department of Education and Science (1985) Education for All (The Swann Report) HMSO Cmnd 9453

Department of Education and Science (1986) Local Authority Training Grants Scheme, Circular 1/86, HMSO

Department of Education and Science (1987a) Educational Provision in the Outer London Borough of Brent, HMSO

Department of Education and Science (1987b) The National Curriculum 5-16, A Consultation Document, DES/Welsh Office

Department of Education and Science, (1987c) Report by HM Inspectors on West Sussex Institute of Higher Education, HMSO

Department of Education and Science (1989a) Future Arrangements for the Accreditation of Courses in Initial Teacher Training — A Consultation Document, HMSO

Department of Education and Science (1989b) Report by HM Inspectors on Responses to Ethnic Diversity in Teacher Training, HMSO

Department of Education and Science (1989c) The Education (Teachers) Regulations, Circular 18/89 (on licensed teachers) HMSO

Department of Education and Science, (1989d) Circular 24/89, Future Arrangements for the Accreditation of Courses of Initial Teacher Training, HMSO

Department of Education and Science (1990a) Standards in Education 1988-89 (HMI Annual Report)

Department of Education and Science, (1990b) Report by HM Inspectors on West Sussex Institute of Higher Education: The Professional Training of Primary School Teachers, HMSO

Department of Education and Science (1990c) Teacher Training a Priority Area — Tim Eggar (News, 29 Nov)

Department of Education and Science, (1992) Reform of Initial Teacher Training, a Consultation Document, HMSO

Dewey, J. (1933) How We Think: A Restatement of the Relation of Reflective Thinking to the Educative Process, Henry Regnery

Dhondy, F, (1974) The Black Explosion in Schools, Race Today, February

Dhondy, F, (1978) Teaching Young Blacks, Race Today May/June pp80-85

Dorn, A. and Hibbert, P. (1987) A Comedy of Errors — Section 11 Funding and Education, in Troyna (1987)

Donald, J. and Rattansi, A. (eds.) (1992) 'Race' Culture and Difference, Sage

Edwards, V (1979) The West Indian Language Issue in British Schools, Routledge Kegan Paul

Epstein, D, (1991) The Birmingham ESG White Areas Project, PHd Thesis, University of Birmingham

Epstein, D (1993) Changing Classroom Cultures, Trentham

Epstein, D (1993) Too Small to Notice? Constructions of Childhood and Discourses of 'Race' in Predominantly White Contexts, Curriculum Studies Vol1, No 3, 1993

Eysenck, H (1971) Race, Intelligence and Education, Temple Smith

Flew, A, (1984) Race, Education and Revolution, Centre for Policy Studies

Fryer, P (1984) Staying Power, Pluto Press

Gaine, C, (1984) What Do We Call People? Multicultural Teaching, Vol 3 No 1, Autumn 1984

Gaine, C and Miller, A (1985) On Race and Gender Stereotyping, Universities Quarterly, Autumn 1985

Gaine, C (1987) No Problem Here, Hutchinson

Gaine, C and Pearce, L (Eds.) (1988) Anti-Racist Education in White Areas, 1987 NAME Conference Report, NAME

Gaine, C (1989) On Getting Equal Opportunities Policies, and Keeping Them, in M. Cole (Ed) Routledge

Gaine, C (1990) LMS and black children, Multicultural Teaching Vol 1X no 1, 1990

Gaine, C (1993) Training for Equality, Longman

Gill, D, (1983) Geography and education for a multicultural society, Commission for Racial Equality

Gill, D. Mayor, B. and Blair, M (1992) Racism and Education, Sage

Gillborn, D (1990) 'Race', Ethnicity and Education, Unwin Hyman

Gillborn, D (1995) Racism and Antiracism in Real Schools, Open University Press

Gilroy, P (1987) There Ain't No Black in the Union Jack, Hutchinson

Giroux, H. and McLaren, P. (1987) Teacher Education as a Counter-Public Sphere... in Popkewitz, T (1987) Critical Studies in Teacher Education, Falmer

Goldsmith's College Communications Group, (1987) Media Coverage of London Councils, Goldsmiths' College, University of London

Gordon, P. (1989) The New Educational Right, Lecture at CARE Conference, London

Gordon, P and Klug, F (1985) Immigration Control — a Brief Guide, Runnymede Trust

Gordon, P. and Klug, F. (1986) New Right, New Racism, Searchlight Publications

Graves, N. (1990) Initial Teacher Education — Policies and Progress, Kogan Page

Grugeon, E. and Woods, P. (1990) Educating All — Multicultural Perspectives in the Primary School, Routledge

Gurnah, A. (1991) Professional Foul or Own Goal? Multicultural Teaching Vol. 9 No. 3, Summer 1991

Hall, S, (1988) Invited Lecture to Dept of Sociology, University of Lancaster

Hall, S (1980) Race Articulation and Societies Structured in Dominance, in UNESCO, Sociological Theories: race and colonialism

Hatcher, R, (1985) Some comments on Mullard's papers for NAME, unpublished

Hatcher, R (1985) On Education for Racial Equality, Multiracial Education Vol 13, No 1

Hatcher, R. (1987) Education for Racial Equality Under Attack, Multicultural Teaching, vol 5, no 3

Hatt, A (1991) Teacher into Tutor, Multicultural Teaching, Vol. 9 No. 3, Summer 1991

Hill, D (1976) Teaching in Multiracial Schools, Methuen

Hill, D, (1989) The Charge of the Right Brigade, Hillcole Group

Hill, D. (1990) Something Old, Something New, Something Borrowed, Something Blue, Hillcole Group

Hill, D. (1991) What's Left in Teacher Education, Hillcole Group

Hillgate Group, (1986) Whose Schools? A Radical Manifesto, Hillgate Group

Hillgate Group, (1986) The Reform of British Education, The Claridge Press

Hillgate Group, (1989) Learning to Teach, The Claridge Press

Hiro, Dilip, (1972) Black British, White British, Penguin

Home Office, (1981) The Brixton Disorders 1981, Report of an Enquiry by Lord Scarman, HMSO Cmnd 8427

Home Office (1989) The Response to Racial Harassment, HMSO

Home Office (1991) Responding to Racial Attacks, HMSO

Honeyford, R, (1982) Multi-racial Myths, TES 19/12/82

Honeyford, R, (1983) Multi-ethnic Intolerance, Salisbury review, no 4 pp 12-13

Honeyford, R, (1984) Education and Race, an Alternative View, Salisbury Review, no 6, pp 30-2

Honeyford, R, (1987) The Swann Fiasco, Salisbury Review, vol 5. no 3, pp 54-6

Honeyford, R, (1988) Integration or Disintegration? Towards a Non-racist Society, Claridge Press

House of Commons, (1981) Racial Disadvantage, Fifth Report of the Home Affairs Committee, HMSO

ILEA, (1983) Race, Sex and Class, ILEA

ILEA, (1985) Education in a Multi-Ethnic Society, an Aide-Memoire for the Inspectorate, ILEA Learning Materials Service

Institute of Education, (1984) Racist Society — Geography Curriculum, Conference Report, Centre for Multicultural Education, London University

Institute of Education Centre for Multicultural Education, (1992) Sagaland, University of London

Institute of Race Relations (1982) Roots of Racism

James, A and Jeffcoate, R (Eds) (1981) The School in the Multicultural Society, Harper and Row

Jeffcoate, R (1979) Positive Image, Readers and Writers/Chameleon

Jeffcoate, R (1981) Evaluating the Curriculum, in James and Jeffcoate, (1981)

Jeffcoate, R (1984) Ethnic Minorities and Education, Harper Education

Jensen, A (1969) Harvard Educational Review, 39, 1-129

Jordan, W. (1968) White Over Black, Penguin

Kelly, E and Cohen, T (1989) Racism in Schools, Trentham

Kirp, D, (1979) Doing Good By Doing Little, University of California Press

Kuper, L (1975) Race, Science and Society, UNESCO/Allen and Unwin

Lane, D, (1987) The Commission for Racial Equality, the First Five Years, New Community, vol 14, nos 1 and 2, pp 12-16

Lane, D, (1988) Brent's Development Programme for Racial Equality in Schools, A Report, London Borough of Brent

Lawlor, S, (1990) Teachers Mistaught, Centre for Policy Studies

Lynch, J (1983) The Multicultural Curriculum, Batsford, 1983

Mac an Ghaill, M, (1988) Young, Gifted and Black, Open University

Macdonald, I et al, (1990) Murder in the Playground, Longsight Press

Macintyre, G (1990) Accreditation of Teacher Education: The Story of CATE 1984-1989, Falmer

Massey, I, (1987) Hampshire Happening: Working Towards Change, Multicultural Teaching, vol 5, no. 2, pp 6-8

Massey, I (1991) More Than Skin Deep, Hodder and Stoughton

Menter, I (1992) The New Right, racism and teacher education: some recent developments, Multicultural Teaching Vol 10 No. 2

Milner, D (1983) Children and Race — 10 Years On, Ward Lock

Modood, T (1990) British Muslims and the Rushdie Affair, Political Quarterly, 61(2) pp 143-60

Modood, T (1992) Not Easy Being British, Runnymede Trust/Trentham

Morrish, I (1971) The Background of Immigrant Children, Unwin

Mukherjee, T. (1981) in The Enemy Within, British Council of Churches

Mullard, C, (1983) Local Authority Policy Documents, A Descriptive Analysis of Contents, Race Relations Policy and Practice Research Unit, University of London Institute of Education

Mullard, C, (1980) Racism in Schools, History, Policy and Practice, University of London Institute of Education Multicultural Centre

Mullard, C, (1981) chapter in Tierney, J. (Ed) (1981) Race, Migration and Schooling, Holt

Mullard, C. (1984) The Three O's, NAME

Mullard, C. (1988) Etharchy: a New Social Formation of Ethnicity, International Sociological Association Conference, Amsterdam

Murray, N and Searle, C, (1989) Racism and the Press in Thatcher's Britain, Institute of Race Relations

Naidoo, B. (1992) Through Whose Eyes? Trentham

Naish, M (1990) Teacher Education Today — in Graves, N (Ed.) (1990) Initial Teacher Education — Policies and Progress, Kogan Page

Nash, I, (1989) Baker Opts for a Team of Moderates, TES, 20/1/89

National Curriculum Council, (1991) The National Curriculum and the Initial Training of Student, Articled and Licensed Teachers, NCC

National Curriculum Monitoring Project, Newsheet no 10, November 1990, Oxford Development Education Unit

National Union of Teachers, (1989) Anti-racism in Education, guidelines, NUT

Naylor, F, (1989) Dewsbury, The School Above the Pub, Claridge Press

Nixon, J (1984) A Teacher's Guide to Multicultural Education, Blackwell

OFSTED (1992) Framework for the Inspection of Schools, HMSO

O'Hear, A, (1988) Who Teaches the Teachers?, Social Affairs Unit

O'Keeffe, D, (Ed) (1986) The Wayward Curriculum, Social Affairs Unit

O'Keeffe, D, (1990a) Equality and Childhood — in Graves, N (Ed.) (1990) Initial Teacher Education — Policies and Progress, Kogan Page

O'Keeffe, D, (1990b) The Wayward Elite, Adam Smith Institute

Open University, (1982) Ethnic Minorities and Education, Open University Course E354, Units 13-14, (Block 4).

Oxford Review of Education, Vol17, No2, 1991 (Special Edition on Equality in Education)

Palmer, F (Ed) (1986) Anti-Racism — an Assault on Education and Value, Sherwood Press

Page, A and Thomas, K (1984) Multicultural Education and the 'All-White' School, University of Nottingham School of Education

Parkinson, J.P. and Macdonald, B, (1972) Teaching Race Neutrally, Race Vol XIII, No 3 pp 299-307

Peters, W (1987) A Class Divided, Yale University Press

Pollard, A and Tann, S. (1987) Reflective Teaching in the Primary School, Cassell

Reeves, F (1983) British Racial Discourse, Cambridge University Press

Reeves, F and Chevannes, M, 1987, (chapter in) Racial Inequality and Education, Troyna, B. (Ed) Tavistock

Redbridge Community Relations Council, (1978) Cause for Concern — West Indian Pupils in Redbridge, Redbridge CRC

Richardson, R. (1983) Match and Mismatch; Conference at London Institute of Education, June, 1983

Richardson R. (1985) Each and Every School, Multicultural Teaching, Vol 3. No. 2, Spring 1985

Rose, E (1969) Colour and Citizenship, OUP/IRR

Runnymede Trust, (1983) Different Worlds, Runnymede Trust/Borough of Lewisham

Runnymede Trust (1993) Equality Assurance, Runnymede Trust/Trentham Books

Runnymede Trust (1994) A Very Light Sleeper, Runnymede

Runnymede Trust (1994) Multi-ethnic Britain: Facts and Trends, Runnymede

Rushdie, S, (1982) The New Empire Within Britain, New Society 9/12/82

Sarup, M. (1986) The Politics of Multiracial Education, Routledge

Schon, D. (1983) The Reflective Practitioner, Temple Smith

Schools Council, (1982) Multicultural Education, Schools Council, York

Scruton, R. (1984) The Meaning of Conservatism, Macmillan

Searle, C. (1977) The World in a Classroom, Writers and Readers

Searle, C (1989) Your Daily Dose — Racism and the Sun, CPBF

Sharma, S. (1987) Education for All on Wheels, Multicultural Teaching, vol 5, no. 2, pp 13-16

Shaw, B (1986) Teacher Training: the Misdirection of British Teaching in O'Keeffe, D, (Ed) (1986) The Wayward Curriculum, Social Affairs Unit

Shaw, K. (1988) in Better to Light a Candle, Perspectives No 39, University of Exeter School of Education

Sikes, P.J. and Sheard, D. (1978) Teaching for Better Race Relations, Cambridge Journal of Education, vol 8, no 2/3

Singh, G, (1988) Language, Race and Education, Jaysons

Smith, D (1977) Racial Disadvantage in Britain, Penguin

Smith, D and Tomlinson, S (1989) The School Effect — A Study of Multi-Racial Comprehensives, PSI

Stenhouse, L. (1975) An Introduction to Curriculum Research and Development, Heinemann

Stenhouse, L. et al, (1982) Teaching About Race Relations, Routledge

Stone, M (1981) The Education of the Black Child in Britain, Fontana

Straker-Welds, M (ed.) (1984) Education for a Multicultural Society, Case studies in ILEA Schools, Bell and Hyman

Taylor, M (1979) Caught Between? NFER Nelson

Taylor, M (1987) Chinese Pupils in Britain, NFER/Nelson

Taylor, M (1992) Equality After ERA? NFER

Taylor, M with Hegarty, S (1985) The Best of Both Worlds? NFER/Nelson

Taylor, W. (1990) The Control of Teacher Education — in Graves, N. (1990) Initial Teacher Education — Policies and Progress, Kogan Page

Times Educational Supplement, (1991a) Pierced by Shrill Complaint, 15th Feb

Times Educational Supplement, (1991b) Nellie and Ken know what's best, 18th Oct.

Todd, R, (1990) Education for a Multicultural Society, Cassell

Tomlinson, S (1990) Multicultural Education in White Schools, Batsford

Tomlinson, S and Coulson, P (1988) Descriptive analysis of a selection of Education support Grants Projects, University of Lancaster

Troyna, B, (1982) The Ideological and Policy Response to Black Pupils in British Schools, In Hartnell, A. (Ed.) (1982) The Social Sciences in Educational Studies, Heinemann

Troyna, B and Williams, J (1986) Racism, Education and the State, Croom Helm

Troyna, B, (Ed) (1987) Racial Inequality and Education, Tavistock

Troyna, B and Hatcher, R (1992) Racism in Children's Lives, Routledge

Van den Berghe, P (1967) Race and Racism, Wiley

Verma, G (1989) Education for All, A Landmark in Pluralism, Falmer

Verma, G. and Bagley, C. (Eds.) (1979) Race, Identity and Education, Macmillan

Warnock, M (1988) A Common Policy for Education, OUP

Watson, J (1979) Between Two Cultures, Blackwell

Willey, R (1982) Teaching in Multicultural Britain, Schools Council

Wright, C (1987) (chapter in) Racial Inequality and Education, Barry Troyna (Ed) Tavistock

Wright, C. (1992) Race Relations in the Primary School, David Fulton

Index